Minneapolis, Minnesota 55404

Power, Property, and History

Barnave's *Introduction to the French Revolution* and Other Writings

Translated, with an Introductory Essay
by
EMANUEL CHILL

A TORCHBOOK LIBRARY EDITION
Harper & Row, Publishers
New York, Evanston, San Francisco, London

Acknowledgements

An earlier and shorter version of the introductory study was delivered before the Columbia University Seminar on Political and Social Thought in April, 1969, and I am indebted to its members for valuable criticisms and suggestions. I am also most grateful to my colleagues, Martin Fleisher, Julian Franklin, Joan Gadol, Walter Struve, and Martin Waldman for their careful readings of the present version. Whatever its failings, these are, of course, my responsibility, not theirs. My translations were conscientiously reviewed by Leonore Loft. Donald Petty of the City College library was unfailingly helpful with inter-library loans. Finally and above all, it was the generous and sympathetic encouragement given by Elsie Chandler which made my work possible.

E. C.

POWER, PROPERTY, AND HISTORY

Copyright © 1971 by Emanuel Chill. All rights reserved. Printed in the United States of America. No part of this book may be used or reproduced in any manner without written permission except in the case of brief quotations embodied in critical articles and reviews. For information address Harper & Row, Publishers, Inc., 49 East 33rd Street, New York, N.Y. 10016. Published simultaneously in Canada by Fitzhenry and Whiteside Limited, Toronto.

First TORCHBOOK LIBRARY EDITION published 1971

LIBRARY OF CONGRESS CATALOG NUMBER: 77-147078

STANDARD BOOK NUMBER: 06-131556-7

Contents

Introduction: Barnave as Philosophical Historian ... 1

- Barnave's Role in the French Revolution ... 4
- The Genre of Philosophical History ... 16
- Aristocracy and Democracy ... 22
- Violence and Progress ... 28
- Barnave and Eighteenth-Century Culture ... 35
- The Sense of Modernity and the Idea of the Past ... 44
- Barnave, Marx, and the Bourgeois Revolution ... 56

Barnave's *Introduction to the French Revolution* ... 75

- I. General Point of View ... 75
- II. That Which Produces the Form of Governments ... 76
- III. General Application of These Ideas from Feudal Government to the Present ... 77
- IV. Application of These Ideas to Ancient States ... 83
- V. Application of the Same Ideas to Modern Europe ... 84
- VI. Development and Proof of the Preceding by Examples and Facts ... 86
- VII. Consequences to Religion of the Progress of Civilization ... 95
- VIII. Democratic Influences: The Italian and Flemish Republics ... 98
- IX. General Ideas on the Republics of Europe ... 100
- X. General Ideas on Monarchies ... 106
- XI. Application of the Preceding to the Inland States of Europe and to the Maritime States ... 112
- XII. Immediate Causes Which Occasioned the French Revolution ... 122

XIII.	Combined Influences Which Were to Act on the Revolution	128

Appendix: Selections from Barnave's Notebooks		133
1.	Of the Moral Sciences Among the Ancients and the Moderns	133
2.	Of the Errors of Men and Peoples	134
3.	Right and Fact	135
4.	Of Reason	136
5.	Influence of the Philosophical Sect on Literature in General	137
6.	J.-J. Rousseau	138
7.	Revolution and Morals	141
8.	Commerce and National Interests	141
9.	Of the Effect of Commerce on Governments	142
10.	Of Taxation	144
11.	Of the Public Debt	146
12.	Of Governments That Hoard	148

Introduction:
Barnave as Philosophical Historian[1]

Joseph Barnave was a leading figure of the Constituent Assembly of 1789–91 and one of its most famous orators. This was his nineteenth-century reputation. Early in the present century, the prominent socialist politician and historian Jean Jaurès (in his *Histoire Socialiste de la Révolution Française*) drew attention to Barnave's posthumously published papers and showed him to be also a thinker of some consequence. Tracing the prehistory of the bourgeois revolution in the various regional economies, Jaurès stops at Dauphiné, Barnave's province, noting the density and strength of its economic life and the fact that its industrial bourgeoisie was more powerful than in any other region. These realities, Jaurès held, lay behind the revolutionary

1. Bérenger de la Drôme's *Oeuvres de Barnave* (Paris, 1843), 4 vols., remains the only such collection (hereafter cited as *Oeuvres*). Volume I includes the *Introduction à la Révolution Française* along with Barnave's account of his parliamentary career, more or less integrally reproduced from one of his notebooks, but with numerous minor errors and substitutions. The other three volumes are not much more than a serious culling of fragments from Barnave's other notebooks, arranged mostly under the editor's own rubrics according to his notions of what was sound and serious. (See F. Vermale, *Manuscrits et éditions des oeuvres de Barnave,* Annales historiques de la Révolution Française, vol. XV, no. 85 [January-February 1938], pp. 75–77.) Bérenger's edition, therefore, should be used only with the greatest caution. I have compared the materials in this edition with facsimile copies of Barnave's eleven notebooks, the originals of which are in the municipal library of Grenoble (U. 5. 216), and corrected them accordingly.
A much more accurate (and accessible) edition of the *Introduction* as well as some interesting selections from Barnave's other notebooks has been prepared by Fernand Rude, *Barnave: Introduction à la Révolution Française,* Cahiers des Annales, no. 15 (Paris, 1960). Bérenger's volumes also include a selection of speeches and other printed materials, as well as some letters, the latter supplemented (and corrected) by Georges Michon's *Correspondance inédite de Barnave en 1792* (Paris, 1924).
A critical edition of Barnave's writings, including materials in the Archives Nationales as well as in Grenoble is badly needed.

initiatives of the provincial estates of Dauphiné in 1788.[2] Jaurès saw Barnave's *Introduction to the French Revolution* (1792–93?) as a theoretical elaboration of the situation, and even consciousness, of this progressive sector of the revolutionary bourgeoisie "whose whole thought he clearly expressed." Jaurès pointed up the realism and political clarity of the bourgeoisie and its young interpreter and recognized in the latter's economic interpretation of the revolution a "prelude to the Marxist interpretation of history" and a "first sketch of economic materialism." Of course Barnave's relation to the bourgeois world determined the limits of his analysis, his "inability to see beyond private property, his failure, despite his superior culture, even to pose the problem of the proletariat."[3]

Such interest as Barnave the thinker has received in our time is traceable to Jaurès' typically cogent and magistral presentation, and it may be said that for the most part this interest has remained within the terms suggested by Jaurès: Barnave's *Introduction* is seen as an illustration of social history, or as a document of the revolutionary bourgeoisie, or, on a somewhat more speculative level, as a bourgeois forerunner of the Marxian idea of class struggle.[4] These lines of inquiry are valid enough insofar

---

2. For a rich account of these realities see Pierre Léon, *La Naissance de la Grande Industrie en Dauphiné* (Presses Universitaires de France, n.d.), I.

3. Jean Jaurès, *Histoire Socialiste de la Révolution Française*, vol. I, *La Constituante* (Paris, 1922), pp. 119–30, "Barnave et la théorie économique de la Révolution."

4. Harold Laski devoted a number of pages to Barnave's *Introduction* in *The Rise of European Liberalism* (London, 1936), accurately summarizing its main arguments and suggesting the "affiliation of ideas" between his speeches and the post-Restoration liberalism of Benjamin Constant and Royer-Collard. Laski sees Barnave as a spokesman of the bourgeoisie, and while recognizing the "superb insight" of his historical analysis, regrets his failure to perceive the proletariat or to "conceive a revolution which goes beyond that in which he participated with such distinction" (pp. 230–36). F. Rude's "Présentation" in his edition cited above (p. 1, n. 1) offers a somewhat more rounded appreciation of the *Introduction* proper. John Lough, "Barnave and the French Revolution," *Modern Quarterly* II, no. 1 (January 1939), 68–78, attempts to interpret the *Introduction* through Barnave's class alignment and political career, noting an "obvious" connection between his role in the Revolution and the strengths and weaknesses of his view of history. The weaknesses re-

as they provide material for other subjects, but they involve Barnave's thinking in a somewhat casual and foreshortened way. Thus most students of Marxism tend to ignore his interest in Montesquieu; in such questions as luxury, international politics,

sulted from the "contradiction" that Barnave himself recognized the class conflict within the Revolution while his *Introduction* "deliberately" ignored it, and this because Barnave could not see beyond a "bourgeois utopia" (pp. 76–78). Despite the distortion involved in imputing a utopian orientation to Barnave, and the schematism of the interpretation, Lough's discussion is a useful brief account of Barnave's ideas.

Of a completely different class, in both its scope and its penetration, is I. L. Popov-Lensky's *Antuan Barnav i materialisticheskoe ponimanie istorii* [Antoine Barnave and the materialist conception of history] (Moscow, 1924). Popov-Lensky's remains the only book-length treatment of Barnave's thought, and it is apparently a serious piece of work. (Since I do not read Russian, I have had to rely on oral translations of large sections in my judgment of this study.) Popov-Lensky treats the literature fully; he offers imaginative and discerning interpretations of Barnave's career and spiritual development. With respect to Barnave's thought, he seems interested, not primarily in establishing its eighteenth-century cultural setting, but rather in assessing its place in the development of the social sciences and exploring its relationship to dialectical materialism, both as method and as ontology. Thus he examines Barnave's debt to Helvétius and Condillac, who, he argues, established a methodological materialism in the social sciences, but whose influence worked against materialistic monism and strengthened the tendency toward agnosticism and eclecticism. Therefore Barnave, while seen as a creative thinker in his own right, is understood as a link between eighteenth-century materialism and the ideologues, Saint-Simon, and Comtean positivism. This result emerges from a careful, informed analysis, but in my opinion it tends to oversystematize somewhat Barnave's philosophical notes. Popov-Lensky also ignores his pessimism, his Hellenism, and his historicizing tendency. On the other hand, Popov-Lensky stresses Barnave's "materialization" of history and his doctrine of classes, acutely delineating his important anticipations of Marx and also their differences on the concept of property, social production, and the state. In this connection there is an interesting discussion of the physiocrats and Turgot as contributors to the materialistic interpretation of historical stages, although I feel that the writer tends to slight the real differences between them and Barnave on the idea of progress. Montesquieu's influence is fully appreciated, and Popov-Lensky develops an illuminating discussion of eighteenth-century theories of climatic and geographical influences. These are a few indications of the rich content of Popov-Lensky's study.

The definitive intellectual biography of Barnave remains to be written, but no serious attempt at it can afford to ignore Popov-Lensky's intelligent and widely informed book. (Unfortunately, there appears to be no copy of it in this country.)

and trade; and generally in the intellectual tendencies of his own time. Jaurès himself held that Barnave spoke for the bourgeoisie of the economically advanced southeast—Dauphiné—although there is scarcely a single reference to that region or province in his work. It is not that Jaurès was wrong, but rather that Barnave's writings, including not only the *Introduction* but his other literary remains as well, can be made to disclose a wider range of evidence; that even as a source of social history they can be developed in a fuller and more comprehensive way. Such a development would relate them not only to the political struggles in which he figured, but to the eighteenth-century Enlightenment of which he was both product and critic. In other words his "superior culture," to which Jaurès refers, merits some attention. As for the *Introduction*, although it contains no discussion of method and little learned criticism, it is nevertheless a step, and possibly an important one, in the eighteenth century's appropriation of the "historical world."

Barnave's Role in the French Revolution[5]

Born in 1761, Barnave came from a Protestant family, somewhat obscure in origins, but by the mid-eighteenth century

---

5. The standard political biography remains E. D. Bradby's *Life of Barnave* (Oxford, 1915), 2 vols. The focus of the work is parliamentary, and it has value because of its very full accounts of important debates as well as its extensive quotations from Barnave's correspondence. However, Barnave's political thought is given little systematic attention and his historical ideas none at all. Miss Bradby tended to idealize Barnave, whom she seems to have seen as an upright young Protestant gentleman. Some of her apologetic arguments have been set aside by Alma Söderhjelm's *Marie-Antoinette et Barnave: Correspondance Secrète* (Paris, 1934). For Barnave's important role in the pre-Revolution in Dauphiné, see Jean Egret, *Le Parlement de Dauphiné . . .* , vol. II, *Le Parlement et la Révolution Dauphinoise* (Grenoble, 1942). The best starting point for the Parisian side of the colonial question during the Revolution is G. Debien's fine book, *Les colons de Saint-Domingue et la Révolution: Essai sur le club Massiac* (Paris, 1953). V. Y. Quinney's unpublished dissertation, "The Committee on Colonies of the French Constituent Assembly" (Wisconsin, 1967), is useful on Barnave's involvement in the Santo Domingo question, especially in pointing up his alignment with French commercial interests. By far the shrewdest judgments of Barnave as politician, as well as the best account of his drift toward the Right ("bourgeois resistance") will be found in Georges Michon, *Essai sur l'histoire du parti feuillant: Adrien*

successful and reputable, and easily of the upper bourgeoisie. His mother was connected with the petty noblesse, her forebears having gained that status relatively recently and probably through military service; and she was known for an aggressive assertiveness of her claims to social recognition, from below as well as from above. His father, descended from silk weavers, small traders, soldiers, and finally seignioral agents, was a lawyer of means and reputation and an official of the bar of the Parlement of Grenoble. Barnave himself was educated privately and destined for the bar. In 1783, at twenty-two, as an *avocat* before the parlement, he delivered a ceremonial address based on Montesquieu ("La Nécessité de la division des pouvoirs dans le corps politique") which showed a measure of political boldness and brought his talents to public notice. In 1788 he was in the vanguard of the local "patriots" who violently protested the exiling of the parlement, engineered a self-convocation of the provincial estates with a "doubling of the third," and demanded the summoning of the Estates General. As part of his contribution to these first open defiances of the royal ministry he wrote several anonymous inflammatory pamphlets and became a member of the extralegal "Assembly of the Three Estates" meeting at Vizille, the château of the wealthy merchant and manufacturer Périer.

Early in 1789 Barnave was elected deputy of the commons to the Estates General. He soon became prominent in the negotiations between the orders and by the end of the summer of 1789 clearly emerged as one of the leaders of the Left, with the reputation of a firebrand and revolutionary extremist. Nevertheless, his friendships and political associations were formed (and were to remain) almost exclusively in the liberal aristocracy, particularly the circle around Charles and Alexandre de Lameth, which included the former magistrate Adrien Duport, the duc d'Aiguillon, prince Victor de Broglie, and Laborde de Méréville, member of a famous banking family.

During the constitutional debates in the National Assembly,

Duport (Paris, 1924). See also Alphonse Aulard's nuanced discussion in *Les orateurs de la Révolution: L'Assemblée constituante* (Paris, 1905), pp. 471–510.

Barnave opposed a second chamber as well as the royal claim to an absolute veto and the power of declaring war. In the fall of 1789 he figured prominently in the reorganization of the Jacobin Club (from the Breton Club). His popularity reached its peak in 1790 when, together with his friends Duport and Alexandre de Lameth, he formed the most important oppositional influence in the Constituent Assembly. Only his forensic powers came close to matching the eloquence of Mirabeau (who pursued a brilliant but devious royalist strategy), and in October 1790 Barnave received the honor of election to the presidency of the National Assembly.

By this time he had become deeply involved in defending the status quo in Santo Domingo against the free mulattoes' claim for political rights and their supporters in and outside the assembly, including the Abbé Grégoire, Condorcet, Brissot, and Mirabeau himself. These and many others were members of the Friends of the Blacks (*Amis des Noirs*), an antislavery society which had been organized in 1788. In 1789 Barnave had regarded the very desirability of colonies as an open question. Within a year, however, he was arguing that the retention of Santo Domingo took precedence over the Declaration of Rights. He held that any attempt to extend the Declaration across the color line in Santo Domingo would entail the loss of this richest of all colonies—probably to England, who hypocritically encouraged the philanthropy of the Friends of the Blacks for her own purposes. Although he argued the question on a frankly pragmatic basis, Barnave led the assembly into a series of demoralizing compromises and evasions which ultimately exposed its majority to the attacks of rising radical politicians and redounded to his own isolation and discredit.

Elected to the Committee on Colonies in March 1790, Barnave was to draft most of its proposals and serve as its spokesman. Throughout 1790 the committee was dominated by deputies friendly to French commercial interests, especially in the Atlantic ports which had grown rich on slaving and their legally privileged trading position (*l'exclusif*) in the French sugar islands. The Santo Domingo planters, on the other hand, had initially welcomed the Revolution as an opportunity to secure autonomy, break what remained of the metropolitan trading monopoly, and escape the domination of French commercial capital. In these objectives they were supported by powerful lobbies in Paris (notably the Club Massiac). Meanwhile the free mulattoes (*hommes libres de couleur*) in Santo Domingo, many of them landed slaveowners, aided by the Friends of the Blacks and a few radical deputies in the assembly, had begun to press for political rights in the colony. In this complex situation Barnave claimed to support the interests of French commerce and argued for the essential maintenance of its trading monopoly. Universal free trade, he would write, was excellent in principle, but given France's relative weakness in manufactures and navigation, she would be swamped and her colonial trade ruined by free competition. Therefore the survival of the state, and indeed of the Revolution itself, required the holding of Santo Domingo for a generation or more.[6] Because of the revolutionary situation and the distrust of the king's ministers, the monopoly could not be enforced by arms. Therefore Barnave, with the support of the Committee on Colonies and of the assembly throughout 1790, tried to defend French commercial privileges by placating the white colonists on other questions, granting them considerable local autonomy, and finally tacitly acceding to their violent measures against the political enfranchisement of the free mulattoes. In thus giving the planters a free hand he may have gone beyond the necessities of the situation; and if this is so, his failure of political objectivity probably resulted from his personal associations with some of the big planters, notably the Lameths.[7]

6. *Oeuvres* II, 199, 208–9.
7. Jaurès wrote that the question of the planters' internal autonomy was Barnave's "decisive moment. Had he really been a statesman, he would have imposed the necessary compromise on his friends of the Hôtel Massiac, or spoken out violently against them." *Histoire socialiste* . . . vol. II, *L'oeuvre de la Constituante*, p. 218. See also Albert Mathiez, *The French Revolution* (New York, 1964), p. 124, and Georges Lefebvre, *The French Revolution: From Its Origins to 1793* (New York, 1962), p. 172.

Slavery as such and the slave trade were never open questions in the Constituent Assembly. Despite a measure of genuine idealism behind the Declaration of Rights of Man and the Citizen, and the relative absence of color prejudice in France, the otherwise conflicting commercial and colonial interests were unanimous on the necessity of slavery. Thus the assembly mainly preserved an embarrassed silence on these subjects.

By the spring of 1791, Barnave and his friends were faced with a new opposition from their left. During 1790 the big planters' Club Massiac and the lobbying deputies of the provincial chambers of commerce had exercised the prevalent influences; now the propaganda of the Friends of the Blacks penetrated the Jacobin societies, and the radicals were able to win a temporary legislative success in the assembly (May 15, 1791). Although Barnave managed to reverse even this limited concession to the mulattoes in the closing days of the Constituent Assembly (September 24, 1791), it was a pyrrhic victory. A month earlier the slave population of Santo Domingo had begun a massive uprising which would finally result in the devastation and loss of the colony. Moreover, assuming that the planters had maintained their dominance, it is doubtful that they would have continued to accept the mother country's commercial monopoly, even in return for a free hand in the island, as Barnave had hoped.

Thus the colonial question involved him in what we can now see was a hopeless cause, and what was apparent at the time: his greatest political failure. He himself traced his loss of popularity to Santo Domingo.

The issue as he repeatedly defined it—candidly, tenaciously, perhaps brutally—had been the choice between philanthropy and national advantage, between abstract principles generally accepted and necessary prudence. But the very prudence of conceding internal control of the colony to the white planters was (and remains) open to question. Barnave's version of the alternatives tended to oversimplify and thus obscure the actual situation in the colony, while at the same time according with the assembly's unstated wish to postpone and avoid consideration of the color question. On the other hand, his rigorous separation of principle and prudence also expressed Barnave's own temperament and talents: a certain hauteur and pride of intellect, and an unmatched capacity for ordering complex materials through sober and positive analysis. This capacity is exemplified in his work in philosophical history; it also created his specific reputation as one of the leading voices of the Constituent Assembly—compellingly informed, comprehensive, ruthlessly logical (but, as Mirabeau said, "without divinity"). Barnave was inclined perhaps to capitalize oratorically on this reputation by becoming the assembly's oracle of "hard" truths; and it may be said that as a politician his cultivation of realism and his cold disdain for "speculative enthusiasms" could at times obscure, even to himself, the weakness and unsoundness of his own position. Tenuous calculations and ramshackle adjustments mark his persistence well beyond the margin of prudence—not without a certain cool gamesman's courage—in support of desperate causes: not only that of the Santo Domingo planters but, in 1791, oligarchical rule in France.

The internal dynamic of the Revolution was even more important than the colonial question in determining Barnave's political fate. Even as early as November 1790 his ascendancy and that of his friends Adrien Duport and Alexandre de Lameth (the "triumvirs") was waning. Their authority in the Jacobin Club dwindled, and there were signs of indirect relations between them and the court—only partially obscured by Barnave's "popular" attacks on the émigrés and the refractory clergy.[8] By the spring of 1791, rising popular agitation in Paris, including labor unrest, was persuading the triumvirs that the Revolution would have to be stabilized through a political mobilization of the wealthy propertied class and even attempts to win the adherence of some of the émigrés and refractory priests. This new course turned on the idea of a strengthened monarchy and, in practice, collaboration with the court. The death of Mirabeau (April 2, 1791) seemed to open the way for such a collaboration;

8. Michon, *Essai*, pp. 83–85.

but the relations that actually developed were to reflect the weaknesses of both parties rather than any real possibility for the kind of strong monarchy based on upper-middle-class opinion which the triumvirs envisaged. The king saw Barnave and his friends as replacing Mirabeau as an adjunct for manipulating the National Assembly; but he ultimately and secretly placed his hopes on an armed congress of the European powers to overawe the revolutionaries and restore his position. On their part the triumvirs, although free of the venality that attached to Mirabeau, must have been impelled toward the cause of order by their loss of influence with the Left and the hope of recouping their power, or at least their influence, in the king's ministry.

Barnave's drift to the right corresponded to a similar movement in the assembly which produced the Chapelier law. This measure, aimed at workers' associations in the name of economic liberty, was also intended to curb the popular societies and political agitation in the Paris sections, and formed part of a general program of conservative bourgeois resistance which emerged in May and June of 1791.[9] It was not the king's flight (June 21) and its pathetic failure that converted Barnave to the royalist cause, as is sometimes held, by arousing his personal sympathy for Marie Antoinette and inspiring her confidence in him (he was one of the three deputies charged with accompanying the royal family back to Paris). There was doubtless a certain chivalrous or romantic tendency in Barnave's character, but he was not one to confuse personal and political objectives. Barnave and his friends saw in the humiliation of the king and his suspension an opportunity to strengthen their influence, to force constitutional monarchy on him, and to curb the new leaders of the Left: Pétion, Grégoire, Robespierre, Brissot, and so on. Such hopes—and fears—led to the formation of the Feuillants in July 1791, a club of the constitutional Right aiming at rallying the resistance of the wealthy middle class to the popular movement.

By this time Barnave seemed to have regained his ascendancy

---

9. Ibid., pp. 201, 203.

in the National Assembly. On July 15 he carried the day with his greatest speech, urging the principle of the king's inviolability and Louis' ultimate restoration, presenting powerful arguments for conservative constitutionalism (which would find many echoes under the July monarchy). Barnave imputed republican sympathies to the Left, and the speech allows us a glimpse of a pessimism grounded not only in "hard" realism, but also in genuine historical insight:

> Some men, seeking perhaps to make of politics a kind of novel-writing, seeking to give us examples from another hemisphere, have seen in America a people occupying a large territory, with a sparse population, without neighboring powers . . . with all the simplicity . . . and sentiments of a young people, given almost completely to agriculture or other simple occupations (*travaux immédiats*) which render men natural and pure, removing those artificial passions which cause revolutions in governments.[10]

These men, he said, opponents of royal inviolability, conclude that the American republic is suitable for us. But they ignore our immense population, our large number of "people exclusively occupied with mental speculation which arouses the imagination and leads to ambition, love of glory. . . . " Foreign rivals however oblige us to form a "single mass." These circumstances are "positive," not dependent on our will. Monarchical government is the only sound course. Republicanism means a weak federative government, finally dominated by aristocracy. An unchanging power must be placed at the center, capable of resisting ambition and the "shocks, rivalries, the vibrations of an immense population, agitated by all the passions spawned by an old society."[11]

The assembly has established liberty and equality. Any further prolongation of our "revolutionary fever," Barnave warned, would be "disastrous," involving not only the end of

10. J. Mavidal and E. Laurent, *Archives parlementaires, première série: 1787–1799*, 82 vols. (Paris, 1868–92), XXVIII, 326.
11. Ibid., p. 329.

the monarchy, but also—what speculative politicians cannot foresee—an attack on property.[12]

> ... is there any remaining aristocracy but that of property? [Revolutions are not made by metaphysical maxims] which deceive some cloistered thinkers, a few men learned in geometry ... who are doubtless nourished by abstractions ... but the multitude ... is won only by realities, is moved only by palpable advantages. ...
>
> You all know that the night of August 4th [1789, when the assembly renounced feudal privileges] gave the Revolution more arms than all the constitutional decrees; but for those who would want to go further, what night of August 4th remains to be made except laws against property?[13]

Thus Barnave, defining the essential, the defensible Revolution as that of the propertied, turned from movement to order. Three days later, hours after the massacre of the Champ de Mars, he commended the municipality and the National Guard of Paris for their quick action;[14] the approval of the assembly showed a majority ready for the harshest measures against the antiroyalist popular movement. The forceful suppression and dispersion of the radicals appeared to be successful. Thus Barnave was encouraged to lead an effort for a conservative revision of the constitutional decrees, involving a further restriction of suffrage, the right of deputies to reelection, and their ministerial eligibility.

The full success of the program depended on rallying the Right, including the diehards of aristocracy. However, they withheld their support, since many of them hated the young firebrands of 1789. Fundamentally the court and Marie Antoinette in particular shared this attitude.

Barnave had entered into a secret correspondence with the queen after the flight to Varennes, hoping to reconcile her to the destruction of aristocratic privileges and convert her to the

12. Ibid.
13. Ibid., p. 330.
14. Ibid., p. 402 (speech of July 18, 1791).

INTRODUCTION: AS PHILOSOPHICAL HISTORIAN 13

constitution. Through her he thought her brother, Emperor Leopold II, could be persuaded to recognize and thus help stabilize the Revolution.[15] But Marie Antoinette played a double game, conducting an even more secret correspondence with Vienna in which she repudiated the Feuillants as well as the constitution and worked for an Austrian intervention. Barnave's relations with the queen were widely suspected in the assembly, where he had already lost much of his popularity and authority in the colonial debates. Thus his isolation increased, while the Feuillants fell to ineffectual bickering. Barnave's realism, which he was wont to contrast with the "chimeras" of the assembly's new Left was itself now enveloped in illusions: that the aristocratic penchants of the court could be suppressed, that the present king could be turned into a popular chief who would dominate the legislature through able and strong Feuillant ministers, that the assembly could be managed so as to clearly support this program, and finally, that these objects could be promoted through his epistolary advice to Marie Antoinette, who privately referred to the Feuillant leaders as "beggars" (*gueux*).[16] In August these illusions were rudely punctured when the triumvirs' attempts to restore the eligibility of deputies for reelection and for ministerial offices were defeated in the assembly. The secret correspondence now begins to show more tergiversations on the queen's side, and finally more forced optimism and frustration on Barnave's.[17] In fact, his political rout and discredit were complete.

(Through the publication of this correspondence, we now know that he lied in his flat and forceful denial of any relations with the royal court at his trial before the Revolutionary Tribunal. This lapse, unusual for him, was certainly not dictated by the hope of exculpating himself legally, for he knew that his trial was political and his condemnation a foregone con-

---

15. Letter to the queen, July 21, 1791. A. Söderhjelm, ed., *Correspondance secrète*, pp. 51–53; also passim.
16. Letter to Fersen, January 4, 1792, quoted ibid., p. 223n.
17. Notably in his letter to the queen of December 14, 1791, among others. Ibid., pp. 210 ff.

clusion, but probably by a kind of political shame at having been the dupe of the queen's manipulations.)

For a few months after the dissolution of the Constituent Assembly on September 30, Barnave remained in Paris, maintaining his correspondence with the queen and some connections with the leaders of the Feuillants, activities of which he must have recognized the growing futility. In January of 1792 he retired to Dauphiné, where he preserved, as far as can be seen, a correct and loyal attitude to the Revolution. He enrolled as an officer in the local national guard and gave himself to study and correspondence. Most of his old friends had joined the "aristocrats" and emigrated, but he was impressed by the unity of revolutionary sentiment among all classes and by the absence of the factional conflicts which marked the development of the revolution in Paris. "Here the distinctions between moderate and extreme patriots (*patriotes enragés*) are of small importance . . . the great division of aristocrats and patriots effaces all others. . . . "[18] The relatively naïve revolutionary consciousness which he found in Dauphiné, and his newly-won distance from the political arena (and from the "whirlpool of vanity and intrigue" which had seized him) probably helped him to refocus his talent for realistic and positive analysis which had been so badly deflected during the last months of the assembly. As always, he favored a conciliatory but firm attitude toward the European powers, especially Austria, regarding her as a natural ally whose support could be won for a constitutional monarchy in France. Naval and colonial expansion were rational tendencies for France, politically as well as economically, since navies would not tempt the monarchy toward military despotism as did large armies.[19] He opposed the drift toward war, holding that partial reverses would do nothing to stabilize the Revolution, as some maintained, and that defeat would be socially disastrous. However, when war came in April of 1792, he urged support of

18. Undated letter, probably written toward the end of January 1792. Michon, *Correspondance inédite*, p. 56.
19. *Oeuvres* I, 183–92.

the Brissotin (or Girondin) ministry on an opportunist basis. Brissot himself had been one of Barnave's bitterest foes and Barnave regarded his followers as "metaphysicians" at best, or ambitious "journalists." Still, he felt that the Brissotins were more dangerous out of power than in, that if they were given the government they would either acquire a sense of national responsibility or, what was more likely, reveal their own dilettantism and incompetence, and so pave the way for the return to power of a consolidated Feuillant party. Barnave's views, expounded in letters to his friends, especially Duport and the Lameths, apparently produced some coolness on their side, for they were actively engaged in a struggle with the Left and the Brissotin ministry and tended to take an increasingly reactionary view of things.[20]

As for the war itself, Barnave predicted that it would be a protracted one, with initial reverses for the French, but ultimate successes as the spirit and discipline of the armies were strengthened. He foresaw that military leaders would play a bigger political role. Nevertheless, war entailed unforeseeable consequences. It was folly to imagine, as many Feuillants now did, that conflict could be limited so as to benefit the king and render the constitution more conservative by enabling him to "mediate" between the national legislature, on the one hand, and the émigrés backed by an armed congress of the powers on the other. "A constitution is very naturally made by a compromise after a civil war, for then the different parts of the social body treat with one another, and that is in some sort a way of discussing it. But a constitution cannot result from a compromise with the foreigner."[21]

In the letters and notebooks of his retirement one senses a tacit recognition, which was also a kind of self-illumination, of the real obstacles on which his policy of resistance in 1791 had foundered—not venal, self-interested journalism, as he had often

20. Michon, *Essai*, pp. 383, 404.
21. Quoted and translated from a notebook in the Archives Nationales (W. 15, *registre* ii, 14) by Bradby, *Life* II, 287.

averred, but aristocracy, which with its republican façade was and remained the enemy, and which had yet to measure its full strength against what he calls democracy.[22] These ideas will be developed later; suffice it to say here that his openness to political realities in the spring and summer of 1792 prepared the ground for the longer view of the Revolution which is the basis of the *Introduction*.

The fall of the monarchy in August 1792 soon led to the discovery in the Tuileries of what was alleged to be evidence of Barnave's improper relations with the court. He was arrested on August 19, imprisoned, finally brought to Paris, tried before the Revolutionary Tribunal, and guillotined in November 1793, at the age of thirty-two.

The Genre of Philosophical History

The *Introduction* was probably written during his year of imprisonment (or at any rate, shortly before it). Such study and writing had been Barnave's practice in his earlier youth during the 1780's, and a number of his notebooks, filled with literary, historical, and philosophical notes and reflections, date from that period.[23] Barnave clearly delighted in study and in the intellectual discipline of steady writing. The *Introduction* should be seen, first of all, as an expression of these traits. Unified by a remarkably coherent structure and an expository development of considerable dramatic power, it is nevertheless not a polished work, nor in any strict sense a scholarly one. Most of the chapter divisions and heads, as well as the full title itself, were supplied

---

22. See, for example, the interesting quotations of his ideas about a second chamber, ibid., 288.
23. I have included what are probably a few of these earlier writings in the Appendix. The other fragments I have selected—of a political, economic, or historical character—are clearly ancillary to the *Introduction* and were probably written in 1792 or 1793. In the following discussion, page references to my translations will be given in parentheses in the text.

by the nineteenth-century editor; and the casual orthography and punctuation, the frequent repetitions, the nervous haste of thought show that the *Introduction* (as distinct from the contiguous narrative-memoir) was not intended for the public, or at most was a sketch or first draft. This circumstance freed Barnave for the most part from deference to the declamatory and sentimental style of the day, and allowed a rapid, sober, and logical form of expression which was in any event natural to him. The *Introduction* is, therefore, a documentary rarity: the product of one of the best minds of the Revolution, engaged not so much in apology or defense as in self-clarification.

The work before us belongs to the eighteenth-century genre of philosophical or conjectural history (*histoire raisonnée*, also known as speculative or natural history) in which the human past is reviewed comprehensively, or in what is regarded to be its typical phases, usually from one of the various secular standpoints of Enlightenment thought—utilitarian, empiricizing, anticlerical, or some combination of these. Writers of philosophical histories used the polyhistorical erudition of the seventeenth and eighteenth centuries, as well as the abundant proto-ethnographical literature of the Jesuit missions and exotic travel, and they were at times themselves contributors to erudition and critical scholarship. But philosophical history was not an intrinsically scholarly enterprise—not dedicated to the authentication of documents or the verification of data, but rather to the ordering of existing historical materials from what was deemed a universal or, as Kant said, cosmopolitical point of view. Philosophical history was a popularizing form in that it expressed basic cultural demands of its age, demands not only of accessibility and readability, but that human history be brought into vital (although not necessarily positive) relationship to the new knowledge of other fields, and above all to the ambition of earthly happiness. Generally, the narration of reigns, wars, and politics in the narrow sense is restricted; the ecclesiastical and doctrinal history of Christianity is a subordinate and deprecated concern, overshadowed by efforts at the comparative treatment of myth and religion.

In place of traditional interests the philosophical historians of the eighteenth century turned to such subjects as primitive society; the origin and development of language, of law, of the exact sciences; the investigation of morals, of taste, of luxury, and especially the rise of the mechanical arts and the expansion of commerce. The development of such topics tended to break out of the old conceptual framework of political power in which the state was understood primarily as a system of domination or of formal juridical relations. And, indeed, most exponents of the Enlightenment had explicitly rejected not only the traditional version of history as a providential succession of "empires" (classically embodied in Bishop Bossuet's *Histoire Universelle*), but also the rationalistic explanation of social origins through contract as well. Instead, states now came to be seen in a fuller and more comprehensive way and as interlinked within a broader process of civilization. The old explanations of civilized life, of "civility," as simply the result of political repression or rational administration ("police"), or a founding lawgiver's vision, or even rational agreement among individuals, no longer sufficed. In the enterprise of philosophical history, civility emerges as a learned ordering of behavior, renewed among the individuals of each generation, yet varying according to the circumstances of time and place. An empirical psychology is extended to the historical study of morals, customs, and manners —that is, of collective representations. Attention turns to the conventional, the economic, and generally what were understood as the noncoercive bonds among men, and from such bases the study of the actual forms of political power was profoundly renovated.

The object of all these interests, questions, and investigations was what the eighteenth century called "civil society." Thus, such notions as "savagery," "barbarism," "refinement," "civility," "civilization," "progress of the arts," "rude and polished nations," became basic themes of philosophical history. Prominent examples of the genre are Voltaire's *Essay on Manners* (1756); a number of the essays in Hume's *Political Discourses* (1752), especially "Of Commerce" and "Of Civil Liberty"; Turgot's

INTRODUCTION: AS PHILOSOPHICAL HISTORIAN   19

"Tableau philosophique des progrès successifs de l'esprit humain" (2nd *Sorbonique*, 1750) and other early writings; Adam Ferguson's *Essay on the History of Civil Society* (1767); John Millar's *Origin of the Distinction of Ranks* (1779); and Condorcet's *Sketch . . . of the Progress of the Human Mind* (1794). Rousseau's *Discourses* (1750, 1755) are doubtless the most famous and consequential instances of speculative or philosophical history, and the fact that they embody (along with much else) a negative judgment on the progress of the arts does not separate them from the genre, since they are a meditation on the course of man's social existence and on the nature of civilization itself (however problematic that concept is for Rousseau). The philosophical histories of the Enlightenment point forward to some of the typical intellectual and learned enterprises of the nineteenth century—to sociology, to the comparative and evolutionary method in the social sciences, and more broadly, to positivism and the theoretical elaboration of socialism. Indeed, *The German Ideology* (1846) of Marx and Engels may be considered as a culminating expression of the philosophical history of civil society, and perhaps the final one, since it raised fundamental questions about the integrity and unity of the very concept of civil society itself.

Barnave was widely read in the historical writing, the jurisprudence, economics, and philosophy of his time, and many of his notebook entries are more or less extended commentaries on his favorite writers: Montesquieu (above all), Voltaire, Helvétius, Rousseau, Adam Smith, William Robertson, Condillac, Mably, and Raynal. Probably Hume and, one would like to think, Ferguson (through Robertson) and Millar as well. Such were the variegated materials which refracted his political experience of the Revolution; for he saw it as a complex historical result, not a drama of edification to be taken en bloc. On the other hand, his own revolutionary vicissitudes helped to open a new perspective on the history of mankind.

The *Introduction* is, then, a philosophical history based on the "natural" tendency of human societies to increase in population and to develop the mechanical arts and commerce. The natural progress of society has been retarded by warfare and conquest and limited by physiographical and climatic conditions; but the basic current of population and industry is, in principle, continuous in any society, although sometimes implicit and, as it were, subterranean. Then in the modern age, in western Europe, the current rather suddenly surfaces and broadens, gathering strength as the "industrious (*laborieuse*) part of the people," the acquirers of commercial property (*propriété mobilière*)—the democracy as Barnave calls them—begin to acquire independence and influence, press against the political "envelope" of society, finally breaking out in the great "explosion" of the French Revolution. As far as I know, Barnave's was the first attempt to link the Revolution with a reasoned account of world history. The Revolution becomes a decisive landmark in the history of civilization; but beyond that, civilization itself is now seen to reveal new contours, and above all a new kind of continuity, from the standpoint of revolutionary crisis.

The continuity which underlies Barnave's presentation is not concretely historical but typological: human societies are ranged into a necessary succession of types or stages: (1) hunting; (2) pastoral; (3) agricultural; (4) industrial-commercial. These stages are mediated by the pressure of numbers and the development of the mechanical arts. The influence of the latter factor seems to preponderate in the higher stages, although Barnave does appear to hold that all increases in population are finally dependent on the progress of the arts, that is, human industry. The hunting and pastoral stages correspond to the distinction (already elaborated by Montesquieu, Turgot, and Adam Ferguson) between savagery and barbarism—that is, in the latter, property distinctions have made their first appearance. Pastoral societies, knowing private possession, also know inequality, if for no other reason than that human slavery, property in men, accompanies property in animals. Thus the natural democracy of the first, gathering or hunting, stage based on the equality of primitive independence disappears under the first form of property, with its accompaniments of inequality, violence, and predatory warfare. But pastoral nomadism presages and to an extent determines the greater inequalities of landed property basic to the third or agricultural stage. Cultivation of the soil represents an advance of the arts but a near-disastrous decline in human freedom. Tied to the soil in a stultifying manner, the cultivator comes increasingly under the domination of large proprietors. Large landholdings either stem from the social rank of the nomadic chiefs at the time of settlement or conquest, or develop in the course of time, due to the nature of a purely agricultural economy. Deeper analysis will show, says Barnave, that agriculture per se, despite its extreme simplicity, is alien to democracy, and especially so where commercial and manufacturing industry have not yet made their appearance. In Rousseau's second *Discourse* the combination of agriculture and metallurgy, by intensifying property relationships of dependence, announced the fall of man into history. For Rousseau's attentive reader Barnave, only this combination can in some measure protect the position of the smallholder. And indeed, it is the dominance of the mechanical arts that finally liberates humanity from its rural idiocy and subjugation.

Barnave's distaste for the agricultural enthusiasms of the eighteenth century is strongly evident and is part of his consistent opposition to physiocracy and its implications. In his historical discussion agriculture bears the violent mark of barbarian nomadic conquerors who bind followers and subjects to newly-won ground. It is therefore the basis of that "strange and anomalous system," feudalism, which sprang up amid the debris of a corrupt and effeminate Roman civilization. In time the "natural course of thing" resumes its sway, and the poor, the industrious (*laborieuse*) part of the people overcomes the feudal anarchy. "The arts, industry, and commerce enrich the industrious class, impoverish the large proprietors." The medieval communes secure their liberties and extend their domination to the local countryside. The Reformation served the same cause: breaking the temporal supremacy of the papacy, which was the keystone of aristocratic power. But the whole Catholic edifice was already in decay, and this is the reason why a single man, Luther, who was by no means a unique figure in the history of the Church, became so dangerous to it. The progress of commercial and manufacturing industry achieved new realizations in the urban republics, and finally in the large monarchies of western Europe. Underlying these changes is the advance of what Barnave calls "democracy."

Aristocracy and Democracy

The foregoing summary shows that for Barnave political and legal institutions express and consolidate various types of social hegemony, and that these in turn rest on specific forms of wealth and property. It is important to note that Barnave makes no place for any contractual origin of political power and that he more or less ignores the question of presocietal man. The crude independence of primitive democracy he derives, not from human nature as such, but from the nature of hunting societies. Herding involves property in animals and men, and hence the emergence of rich and powerful chiefs—aristocracy. Agricultural societies inevitably produce unequal divisions and aristocracies—either moderate, where as in the ancient world they are counterbalanced by commerce, or tyrannical, as under feudalism. The underlying principle of all aristocracy is landed property (*propriété foncière*). The modern world exhibits the progress of the mechanical arts and the gradual extension of industrial and commercial property (*propriété mobilière*) which is the material counterpart of democracy.[24] This is a democracy of the second level, recalling to men of the eighteenth century the primitive independence of the first societies, but resembling it only in an abstract sense of legal equality. Barnave is not interested in following the history of democracy as a political form through the

---

24. Barnave's *propriété foncière* and *mobilière* correspond fairly closely to Marx's distinction between "estate," or "natural" capital, and "movable" capital. Movable capital can be transformed into money. Karl Marx and Friedrich Engels, *The German Ideology* (New York, 1939), p. 51.

small states of antiquity and early modern Europe.[25] He understands democracy proper as the sum of the conditions and possibilities of large commercial societies: easy communications, accumulation of capital, regular taxation, standing armies, public debts, big cities, and colonial enterprises, together with that "boldness and independence of mind which results from the feeling of power." It is the coming into their own of the industrious part of the population, the "poor." (His sense of the word "poor" will be explained below, esp. pp. 56–59.)

Democracy and aristocracy are the two basic forms of organized society. Aristocratic power is exercised directly; social dominance is simultaneously political dominance. Democratic power is more complex. Democracy reanimates the "monarchical principle" which has been latent in primitive society, submerged under the feudal regime, but acquires a certain autonomy as the commons begin to counterbalance the weight of aristocracy—"it raises itself above both." The basis of monarchy is the *"force publique,"* mainly a regular army. Aristocracy means unmediated coercion by landed social power, but democracy requires for its full realization the appropriation of an external, independent social power: monarchy. In the early eighteenth century monarchy ostensibly comes into its own through the balancing of orders or "estates," and this is what Montesquieu took to be monarchy per se: its nature, rule through fundamental laws and a hierarchy of privilege, and its principle "honor." But what Montesquieu took for a definitive totality is only, says Barnave, "a precarious state . . . a passage between two more determinate forms of government; and this was [the core of error in] Montesquieu's doctrine," for although the maxims of honor still reigned for a time, the "real basis" of aristocratic power was

---

25. Barnave's political evaluation of the urban democracies of antiquity is unclear in the *Introduction,* although in one of his last speeches in the assembly he pointed out that classical democracy rested on the slavery of the greater part of the population (*Archives parlementaires,* XXIX, 366; August 11, 1791). Moreover, in the *Introduction* his opinion is definite that the direct democracy which characterized the beginnings of the European urban republics was inherently unstable and thus short-lived.

gone.[26] Even in Montesquieu's time the domination of royal power was held in check, not only by the "memory" of aristocratic power, but also by "opinion which is the prelude to the power of the people." The latter may take the form of a limited monarchy, or (although this is less likely in the great maritime states) may be subverted and contained by the hypertrophy of monarchy: military despotism.

Modern freedom, which for Montesquieu depends on the monarchy's delicate equipoise of authority, law, and rank, is for Barnave the definitive result of modern history—not an arrest or equilibrium of forces, but the natural course of things, wherein the people overcome local power and privilege and appropriate the institutions of monarchy to their own national needs. Such, broadly understood, was the result of English history, and such was Barnave's own political program in the French Revolution, with the difference that he saw no possibility of the French nobility exercising a constructive, conservative function in an upper chamber (in the near future, at any rate). On the other hand, his idea that "democracy" could come into positive relationship with the existing monarchy shows how he distinguished between what he considered a democratic *social order* and democratic *political forms,* rejecting the latter. Of course, a constitutional monarchy required a publicly elected legislature, but he held that its members as well as their propertied electors should be seen as an elite of public functionaries rather than mandatories of their constituents in any strict sense.[27] "The people are sovereign, but in representative government their representatives are their trustees (*tuteurs*)."[28] This theoretical severing of ties between the deputies and their actual constituents was squarely in line with the antidemocratic provisions of the constitution of 1791. Barnave, therefore, did not hesitate to oppose franchise extension, and indeed to argue in 1791 for its further restriction. He took pains to distinguish be-

26. Besides the *Introduction* (infra, p. 111) see *Oeuvres* II, 177–78, "Of the Transition from the Aristocracy of Power to the Aristocracy of Honor."
27. Speech of August 11, 1791; *Archives parlementaires* XXIX, 366.
28. Speech of August 31, 1791; ibid. XXX, 115.

tween democratic and representative *governments*, holding for the latter in its "true character, according to which the well-to-do and enlightened class of citizens must govern the state."[29] The democratic *social* order of commercial property finds its completion in the *political* order of a parliamentary elite.

Barnave, therefore, agreed with the classics of modern political thought in understanding modern freedom as the private individual's ability to pursue private interests in "tranquillity," which is for the "generality of mankind . . . the primary need."[30] Freedom in this meaning does not directly entail civic virtue or responsibilities. Modern men do not live through the state but in it, surrounded by laws and institutions which they can understand objectively and use to their rational benefit as individuals. It is in this sense that Barnave, like Voltaire and Hume before him, was confident in the civilizing (refining, polishing) power of the large modern monarchies, with their disciplined armies and enlarging bureaucracies, increasingly obliged to govern through standing rules, thus providing security and, despite their nature, a favorable setting for the expansion of commerce, wealth, and the "arts"—and ultimately, if hesitatingly, sanctioning the attendant vocational freedom and independence of individuals as well.[31]

As early as the 1740's this confidence had necessitated, among other things, the refusal of the dilemma cynically posed by Mandeville in his *Fable of the Bees* (1714, 1723) of private vices–public benefits. Mandeville had argued (and Montesquieu as well as Rousseau were to agree on their own profounder levels) that the prosperity of commercial societies as such necessitated luxury—mainly private consumption and ostentation—which in turn rested on sharp social inequalities and large reservoirs of poverty. The refusal of this dilemma involved not so much the denial of inequality or poverty as the opening up of an

---

29. *Oeuvres* I, 205.
30. Speech of August 31, 1791; *Archives parlementaires* XXX, 114.
31. Voltaire was the more sanguine (*Siècle de Louis XIV* [1751]). Hume had some doubts, not about centralized monarchies per se, but because of their prevailing aristocratic ethos. See especially his essay "Of Civil liberty" (1752).

historical perspective in which "luxury" could be relativized and divested of its moral opprobrium. (Only then could labor and industry be treated positively.) Luxury, argued Voltaire, Hume, Adam Ferguson, James Steuart, and others, was not necessarily the depraved antithesis of a supposed Spartan simplicity, but rather an empty term which acquired meaning only when related to the wealth and manners of particular societies.[32] One age's "luxury" was another's necessity. In commercial societies, the prospect of abundant and varied luxuries could even spur activity and overcome the older luxury of slothful indolence.

It will be seen that Barnave did not regard the phenomena of modern luxury quite as positively and genially as did Voltaire and Hume, but he certainly accorded with their denial of the revelance of rustic utopias and Spartan idylls—Mandevillian, Rousseauan, or for that matter Christian. Like Voltaire and Hume, he was reconciled (albeit somewhat less optimistically) to the large states of the modern Occident, and therefore suspicious of political nostalgias for golden ages and impossible republics. He believed, as we have seen, that human slavery permeated pastoral societies, that it was general in early stages of society and represented more than the product of local mores and conditions. Convinced that classical culture remained unrivalled in its integrity of life and truth to nature, he nevertheless reminded his republicanizing opponents in the Constituent Assembly that classical democracy had enslaved the majority of the population. The "moderation" of the ancient aristocratic republics which Montesquieu so praised, he would probably have argued depended on the extent to which urban commercial democracy was able to counterbalance and attenuate aristocratic

32. Voltaire, *Le mondain* (1736); see also his *Défense du Mondain* (1737) as well as the approving letter of the political economist Melon, in *Oeuvres complètes de Voltaire* X (Paris, 1877), 83–93. (Melon's *Essai politique sur le commerce* [1735] was an important source of the eighteenth-century rehabilitation of luxury.) Hume, "Of Refinement in the Arts" (1752). Adam Ferguson, *An Essay on the History of Civil Society* (Edinburgh, 1966; 1st ed., 1767), pp. 244–61. James Steuart, *Works* (London, 1805), vol. I, *An Inquiry into the Principles of Political Economy*, pp. 428–31.

power, rather than on political virtue and public freedom. At any rate, the political "virtue" which Montesquieu regarded as the animating principle of republics has little importance in this sober view of history.

Indeed, the validity of republicanism comes in for severe restriction in Barnave's analysis. In part his criticism of republican institutions is merely a continuation of his debate with the Left toward the close of the Constituent Assembly; but it also grows out of a highly original interpretation of the early phase of modern European history, an interpretation which modern students might find instructive still. Barnave links the republics of modern Europe with those of antiquity, not through civic virtue, but through the history of commerce and the arts. The Italian cities, the Flemish and Hanseatic leagues, and the United Provinces represent a further development of commercial and industrial wealth which had arisen in the Mediterranean world. But the European republics, although based on commerce, are nevertheless inherently unstable because of its effects. These small states centered on a commercial town are democracies of industry, the arts; since they lack the military spirit, their republican constitutions are repeatedly endangered by their own military needs. Moreover, such direct democracies, which have lost the primitive simplicity of manners, are prone to intestine violence. The richer citizens make themselves into a mercantile aristocracy, but this is a spurious form which has nothing in common with the older feudal aristocracy. The divisiveness and stratification of these mercantile republics are not, however, inevitable consequences of commercial property per se, but local manifestations peculiar to small states—which states, one may add, dominated the first phase of the commercial revolution. The republics of early modern Europe are, therefore, transitional forms in the development of commercial societies. They lose preeminence to the larger monarchies of western Europe which come into their own in the seventeenth and eighteenth centuries, and provide a more stable, and indeed the definitive, environment of commercial property.

Thus commercial republics are assimilated historically to the more comprehensive concept of monarchy under which industry, equality, and public opinion find their fullest realization. Monarchy is not an abstract type, but the historical convergence of commercial wealth and public force in a large area: "The political force resulting naturally from the enfranchisement and wealth of the people was concentrated in the monarch" (p. 94). Aristocracy and democracy are not generically competitive principles within the body politic, but rather successive historical developments.

Once the [mechanical] arts and commerce have succeeded in penetrating the people and creating a new means of wealth in support of the industrious class, a revolution in political laws is prepared. Just as the possession of land gave rise to the aristocracy, industrial property increases the power of the people; they acquire their liberty, they multiply, they begin to influence affairs [p. 82].

Violence and Progress

While in principle any human society can naturally evolve through the progressive stages of property, and thus finally from aristocracy to democracy, natural possibilities are limited by natural environment. And in fact the Mediterranean and especially the west-European littorals show the influence of sky and land combined to maximize the development of human talent and industry. In this favorable setting the transition from agriculture to industry could occur naturally, with a certain automatism. Barnave had studied the *Wealth of Nations* carefully.[33] He follows Smith in assuming a "natural" economic interdependence of the rising town and surrounding country, and their unity as a market in which the division of labor strengthens the position and independence of both craftsmen and small cultivators (Bk. III, Chap. I). Where this natural symbiosis is thwarted by barbarian conquest and feudal power, he still follows Smith in ascribing the ultimate decay of the landed nobility to its en-

---

33. F. Rude reproduces his notes on the *Wealth of Nations* in his edition of Barnave's *Introduction*, (see p. 1, n. 1), pp. 74–78.

slavement to the new enjoyments held out by the commodity producers of the towns (Bk. III, Chap. IV). Feudalism itself was, however, not only a break in natural continuity but a great social regression. Barnave makes no attempt to account for the necessity of feudalism within the general order of history; he neglects to draw even the usual eighteenth-century contrasts between modern enlightenment and feudal superstition, passing quickly over the latter's "strange regime" of violence and anarchy, and drily noting its repressive and destructive character.

It must be observed that the interpretation of feudalism in Barnave's synthesis does not attain the level already achieved by critical historiography in the eighteenth century. Turgot, although much more intimately committed to the classicizing ideas of the Enlightenment, gave medieval inventions and cultural contributions a much better, or at any rate a more serious, notice.[34] So too did the Scottish thinkers John Millar and Adam Ferguson, in their accounts of the composite influence of chivalry and Christianity on modern taste and morals. Millar is especially notable in this respect. One of the profoundest minds of the Scottish Enlightenment, his learned equipment as well as his sociological grasp were incomparably more powerful than Barnave's. Millar's attentiveness to feudal institutions is all the more notable by contrast to Barnave's neglect, since both saw the same kinds of connections between changing property forms and the growth of social subordination, and Millar's development of the comparative method would otherwise seem to make his work a standard or model for Barnave.[35] But it is above all Montesquieu's *Spirit of the Laws* (1748), which we know Barnave to have read and admired, that points up Barnave's cursory treatment of feudalism, and shows moreover that he was not

34. "Tableau philosophique des progrès successifs de l'esprit humain" (2d *Sorbonique*), *Oeuvres de Turgot*, ed. G. Schelle (Paris, 1913–21), I, 231.
35. John Millar, *The Origin of the Distinction of Ranks* (Edinburgh, 1806), esp. pp. 72–82 on chivalry, and Ferguson, *Essay on . . . Civil Society*, pp. 201–3, for the same. (The original version of Millar's work, *Observations Concerning the Distinction of Ranks in Society*, was published in 1771.)
Ferguson had emphasized the relation between the development of property and social subordination before Millar, but less clearly and systematically.

ignorant of the problem. For the last books (28, 30, 31) of the *Spirit of the Laws* offered a *mise au point* of the existing state of the question as well as an historically dynamic analysis of the origin and development of feudal institutions which was, and in many ways remains, exemplary.

To understand Barnave's relative neglect of feudalism as a social order and as an influence on later periods is probably to understand his most basic political and intellectual orientations. And with respect to these it will not do simply to assimilate them to the Enlightenment's rationalistic and moralizing disparagement of medieval "darkness" (an attitude the strength and consistency of which was, in any event, somewhat overdrawn by nineteenth-century investigators). As will be shown, Barnave, for all his empiricism and materialism, succeeded in attaining a critical and reflective distance from the Enlightenment as a movement. Much more important to him than the literary-philosophical mode would have been the fact that the question of the feudal origins of the Frankish monarchy had been opened up by Boulainvilliers and Montesquieu, exponents of a reactionary aristocratic ideology, whose investigations, however fruitful, were deeply implicated in the *thèse nobiliaire*—the refurbished defense of corporate hierarchy and privilege in the eighteenth century. To the *thèse nobiliaire* Barnave (except possibly for a few sallies in behalf of the Parlement of Grenoble in a pamphlet polemic of 1788) was deeply antipathetic.

But there was probably another, no less powerful reason which kept him from treating feudalism in anything like a rounded or consequential manner, and this had to do with method. Barnave's interpretive procedures do not focus on the persistence beyond their time of political forms per se, or of the higher forms of culture—specifically those feudal continuities and survivals which are essential in Montesquieu's elaboration of the principle of "honor," or which figure in Adam Ferguson's appreciation of the elements of modern manners.[36] Barnave is, of course,

---

36. Or, for that matter, in Tocqueville's account of the influence of the nobility on modern English political culture, the historical substance of his concept of liberty (*The Old Regime and the French Revolution*).

aware that an aristocracy of honor may persist for a time after the demise of an aristocracy of power, but he regards this "memory" as of small historic importance. The significant continuities in human history are not such survivals, but the palpable material ones of population and industry, and their organizing principle is the succession of property forms. Feudalism represents a regressive type of landed property. True, "feudal government" was the "common origin" (*départ commun*) of the various states of modern Europe,[37] but this is meant mainly in the indirect sense that it reinforced the predominance of landed property. With respect to feudal institutions and *moeurs* as such, however, these were *original* only in the sense of providing a general debris or raw material out of which the commercial republics and monarchies were later constructed. For the feudal regime had hardly begun to achieve a certain (anomalous) coherence before it was being cracked and shattered by the rise of the industrious class (*classe laborieuse*).

Barnave seems to picture the rise of this democracy as a process of organic growth; but by using the medical metaphors of humoral congestion, "extravasation," and so on, he points up its historical tendency toward violence. Aristocratic governments, and feudalism especially, are disposed to "certain maladies" which may be occasioned by events insignificant in themselves (like Luther's revolt). In his notes Barnave speaks of times of "plethora" when government can no longer contain this "plenitude" nor the resulting "fermentation," which in turn prepares and may necessitate an "explosion." "Plethora" expresses the social development of democracy, of civil society, for it is constituted of three related elements: "population, wealth, and new ideas." This social content shatters the old order; and this is for him a primarily material process since as he says, the "ideas" are almost "the effect of the fermentation of the two others."[38]

This emphasis on material factors is obviously close to Marx's

---

37. "Préambule" or plan of Barnave's *Introduction*, as reproduced in Rude, *Barnave*, pp. 63–64.
38. "Réflexions sur l'ordre sociale dans ses divers périodes," ibid., pp. 71–72.

view. It is also notable that the parallelism involves larger implications on each side. Marx and Barnave seem to agree that the material continuity of human history is an hypothesis, a formula of possible evolutions, but *not* the basis of a universal history united by technical influences, borrowings, or diffusions. Marx's study notes on precapitalist societies concentrated on the stabilizing and economically conservative elements within particular social economies of the ancient world, and avoided the establishment of definite economic (not to speak of ideational) transitions and successions between them.[39] In his efforts to explain why ancient societies did not develop the institutions of capital and wage labor, one senses also his cautiousness about affirming the general and progressive continuity of material life. Human history is a tenuous affair; the thread of material production is fragile, and indeed repeatedly broken, before men achieve the stage of their self-universalization in modern industry and the world market.[40] (In line with this, it has been remarked that Marx's attention to feudalism was relatively scant and that the Marxian approach to feudalism, in its origins and in the transition to capitalism, is unclear and problematical.[41])

Related to Marx's sense of the tenuousness of man's early social development is his readiness to give the violence of the human past its full due. Typically in early societies, the force of conquest is a productive force.[42] Marx saw plundering violence as woven into the very fabric of ancient societies. More than that, he insisted that the rise of modern bourgeois production had required the forcible expropriation of classes and the conquest of continents ("primitive accumulation"), while the life of modern industry required, for example, a vast system of

---

39. Edited by E. J. Hobsbawm as *Pre-capitalist Economic Formations* (London, 1964), a part of the *Grundrisse der Kritik der Politischen Ökonomie* which Marx wrote in 1857–58.
40. Marx and Engels, *German Ideology*, p. 49.
41. Hobsbawm, *Pre-capitalist . . . Formations*. He also discusses some of the literature in his Introduction, pp. 44–46, 61–63.
42. Ibid., pp. 71, 89.

INTRODUCTION: AS PHILOSOPHICAL HISTORIAN   33

chattel slavery in America. Thus, violence even in its more manifest and traditional forms—that is, apart from class struggle —could not be regarded as something external to civilization, but rather as intimately bound up with its actual course, at least up to the foundations of commercial capitalism.[43] On such grounds, in part, Marx was able to avoid the abstract problems of evil and theodicy and to deny that history "worked providentially" toward equality, and so forth.[44]

Barnave's antiprovidentialism is linked with a comparable treatment of historical violence: plunder, organized warfare, and colonialism enter into the historical process positively, as ineluctable facts. This is far from saying that violence has the same *economic* significance for him as it does for Marx. The latter holds that conquest, if it is to be durable and more than a "taking," necessitates an adjustment of the conquerors' "form of community" (relations of production) to that of the conquered.[45] Barnave verged on this problem in pointing out the regressive effects on Spain of her American conquest (cf. pp. 116–17 of this volume), but he carried the idea no further. Again, Marx wants to show the historical genesis of capitalist production in "letters of blood and fire" which dwarf the "revolting prerogatives" of feudal lordship; but Barnave held that feudal violence was far deeper than that of the modern state; and he had not, moreover, the demystifying intent which animated Marx's account of primitive accumulation. Nevertheless, it is fair to say that neither thinker regards the historical process as observing an economy of human means. Thus Barnave stressed the inherently violent character of pastoral and strictly agricultural societies. Even more widely, for him the historical record is full of wastes, thwartings, regressions: feudalism, the aborted democracy of the Spanish towns in the sixteenth century, the stagnating oligarchical re-

---

43. Karl Marx, *Capital I* (Chicago, 1912), pt. VIII: "The So-Called Primitive Accumulation," e.g., 785, 786, 787, 823, 827, 835, 837.
44. *The Poverty of Philosophy* (New York, n.d.), p. 101.
45. *German Ideology*, p. 62.

publics of early modern Europe. Departing from the consensus of eighteenth-century economic thought, Barnave saw no necessary opposition between war and commerce. Turgot and Condorcet, especially, had assimilated the rise of commerce to the broader category of *communication*, which in turn cemented the rational unity of mankind and enlarged the scope of its peaceful relations. For Barnave, military (and naval) might was not regressive or atavistic per se. True, in commercial republics military power tended to become a social interest threatening to the life of the ruling mercantile oligarchies. But the large modern states were distinguished by their ability to organize and control large armies. (The idea is similar to Hume's.) Of course, in modern societies navies have generally conformed better than armies to the needs and safety of the "industrious class." England was a case in point, and in France's actual situation the Revolution would be more secure if Louis XVI could be kept from control of a large land force. But Barnave's caution about armies was a purely pragmatic judgment, based on France's situation—historical, geographical, diplomatic. Violence is changing, multiform, but deeply embedded in ancient and modern societies.

In the optimistic currents of the eighteenth century, violence was assimilated to passion and ignorance, and hence deemed external to civilization. How vivid Turgot's awareness of the vast darkness embracing ancient societies—of the feudal chaos and anarchy surrounding the flickering genius of the Middle Ages —of invasions, brutalizing conquests! Nevertheless, for him the blind savagery that filled the past, precisely because *external* to genius and human progress, was ultimately the most important instrumentality in the diffusion of that genius and that progress, in the advance of civilization.[46] Not so for Barnave: there is no invisible hand to orchestrate the violent clash of empires and

46. Turgot's idea is that the danger to civilization comes, not from barbarian violence, but from the spirit of routine. "Recherches sur les causes des progrès et de la décadence" (1748), *Oeuvres de Turgot* I, 133, 137. On penumbral barbarism see "Tableau philosophique . . . " (2d *Sorbonique*) and "Plan de deux discours sur l'histoire universelle" (ca. 1751), ibid., pp. 221–22, 284.

races with the progress of civilization in a harmonious order of universal history. (Nor, incidentally, does Barnave see such a hand or such a harmony in trade between the nations.)

Neverthelesss, the modern development of the mechanical arts does tend to abrogate the irrationality of things and expand its immanent order to wider spheres. "The history of modern Europe is what is important to know well. . . ." The advance of commercial property is irresistible in the large maritime states of western Europe, and this advance progressively liberates these states from the accidents of war and conquest. "Moreover, as states become more powerful, the less their inner mode of existence depends on external [political] influences, the more they are themselves . . ." (p. 115). Modern states are interrelated through the European balance of power—for Barnave, a veritable system. Violence does not disappear, but becomes organized force in the form of large standing armies. The economic dimension of military power, especially its cost, comes more into view. Wars are no longer barbarian incursions, less and less expeditions of plunder, more and more outgrowths of colonial and commercial rivalry. A moderate military discipline in the population may even counteract the disposition to luxury. Therefore, the purely destructive effects of violence are diminished in the course of modern history.

But this order rests upon the progress of the mechanical arts, and it is here that we can seize the really significant continuity of human history. We may infer that in Barnave's view of his age this progress has reached such a pitch and generality that thought can for the first time attempt the reconstruction of its historical development and grasp its real effects on laws and institutions.

Barnave and Eighteenth-Century Culture

Such emphasis on the mechanical arts was, of course, very strong in the *Encyclopédie* (1751–65). Indeed, the contributors' attention to the technical instruments of production as such was greater than Barnave's and even Marx's. Nevertheless, the consensus of the historical-sociological articles suggest that the progress of industrial techniques was understood as ancillary to and exemplary of the development of human reason. Moreover the Encyclopedists cleave to the diffusionist idea, assuming the model of rationality to lie in the past, in natural man, or among the wise Egyptians.[47] None of the Encyclopedists who touch on the history of civilization escapes the notion of a primitive natural empiricism which it is the task of a scattered and confused humanity to reconstitute. Turgot, too, shared this diffusionism, not to speak of his belief in Providence.[48] His interest in mechanical invention is an interest in the distribution of individual genius—real, constant, but lost and hidden in barbarous ages.[49] The universalization of progress, its irreversibility, is the work of language and scientific communication, which are themselves the essential content of progress. This notion of the cognitive unity of mankind is all the more apparent in Turgot's disciple Condorcet, whose *Sketch* . . . (1794) foretold the coming epoch, the tenth, dominated by the progress of the human mind—a universalization of science, benevolence, and economic liberty which would progressively diminish all national and social antagonisms and which the philosopher in his garret hiding place cherished as a consolatory truth.

Barnave's prison writings are a much soberer affair. This is not simply a matter of tone or temperament; his resistance to the optimism exemplified by Turgot and Condorcet extends to ideas on the nature of history and to urgent questions such as the nature of international rivalry and the interrelations between economic theory and policy. Although neither Turgot nor Condorcet was a strict adherent of physiocracy—of the *"secte des économistes"* as the school was then known—they actively sympathized with its main political theses: the primacy of agricultural production, involving an acceptance of the existing

---

47. René Hubert, *Les sciences sociales dans l'Encyclopédie* (Paris, 1923), pp. 52–59, 358.
48. *Oeuvres de Turgot* I, 216–17, 284 (the "Tableau" and the "Plan," respectively).
49. Ibid., I, 117, 118 ("Recherches sur les causes des progrès").

facts of landed proprietorship; the necessity and inviolability of private property and its inequality as the basis of all society; the uselessness of colonial and other monopolies; the natural harmony of all social interests, given economic liberty both nationally and, ultimately, internationally; and the ideological corollaries of the foregoing—a certain theoretical disdain for sumptuous courts and capitals, and a belief that political conflicts could become problems of rational administration (Turgot's "legal despotism," Condorcet's social statistics). Barnave was to take issue with most of these ideas.

He had read Adam Smith as well as the *économistes,* and the former's caution of generalization, qualified by historical development and illustration, he certainly found more congenial than the polemics and rigorously framed propositions of the *secte.* Like Smith, he wanted to take account of the interests and rivalries of specific states, and although as ready as any well-read person of his time to admit the long-term validity of free trade and an international division of labor, he was attentive to the relative weakness of French industry and exports, and therefore to the need for colonies and protection—against the English rival above all. Indeed, his appraisal of England illustrates his virtues as a political interpreter. He found the English constitution the "best in the world"; the best adapted, that is, but inapplicable in France (a judgment evidenced by his political position in 1789). He saw important parallels and continuities between the English and French revolutions, both testifying to the power of commerce and "democracy," but deplored the influence of English tastes and ideas in his own nation. Dissenting from the physiocrats (and in this case Hume and Smith as well), he interpreted England's national debt as an important sign and source of her national power—which in turn must concern the French in trade, diplomacy, and war—a prescient view of the international situation, as the next two decades would demonstrate. And, one may add, no less significant as a view of things fundamentally at odds with the pacifist orientation of the physiocrats and their economic liberalism.

Of course, Barnave held for internal free trade and defense of private property; but his whole approach to civil society, comparative and historical, precluded arguments for absolute property rights, even those modified positions based on abstract social utility common among the physiocrats and Turgot. Again, rather than a hypothetical economic harmony within a national economy of big agricultural producers, he perceived the clash, or at least the differentiation of interests, between large landed property and commercial wealth. He believed, like Adam Smith, that in a society permeated by commercial wealth landholdings would become smaller, and that the class of small, industrious husbandmen would increase. Commercial wealth, besides its intrinsic disposition to centralized political power, could give rise to a distinct financial interest directly attached to national unity through its holding of a permanent national debt. Landed proprietors, however enlightened as individuals, tended as a class toward irresponsible military aggression and particularist federal institutions, especially with regard to taxation. Barnave was critical of the decentralizing tendencies of the constitution of 1791, and he associated them with the landed interests, the nobility, as well as their unwitting adjuncts, the ambitious politicians of the rising Left. Moreover, as against the rural ideologies of the eighteenth century which, aided by Rousseau's inspiration, spread far beyond their physiocratic core of analysis, he emphasized the cultural and economic importance of large and opulent capital cities. Generally it may be said that Barnave's doubts about eighteenth-century optimism centered on the system-building of the economists and their grand improving projections, as well as on the Rousseauan culture of rusticity, inward innocence, and the primary sentiments (two trends of thought which had anyway become complexly interwoven).

Barnave's skeptical realism was not a matter of thought alone: it also reflected some of his political associations and friendships—certainly with J. J. Mounier, an early émigré but his colleague in the leadership of the Dauphiné revolution in 1788 and a close student of history and of the English constitution. Certainly also with the jurist Adrien Duport, reputedly the "brains" of the triumvirate; probably with the colonial traders and with the banker Laborde de Méréville. On the other hand, his doubts about the special optimisms of the age were ultimately reinforced by his confrontations with the rising Left of 1791 and its revolutionary universalism. This Left, including a few deputies such as Robespierre, Grégoire, Pétion, and Buzot, formed a loose network of friendship and influence centered around the journalist J. P. Brissot and the salon of Madame Roland. The latter was an ardent devotee of Plutarch and Rousseau, and Brissot had traveled in America, dabbled in legal reform, written a confused book on the naturalness of property rights, been an agent of the duc d'Orléans, and played an important part in the antislavery movement. But the real intellectual of the Brissotin grouping was Condorcet himself. To him Barnave would not have hesitated to extend his opinion of the economists generally: "fanatics, sectaries, enthusiasts of a few principles which they apply without regard to circumstances and without restriction." Brissot he thought a "hypocrite of philosophy, as others are of religion."[50]

Barnave's stinging comments on the Brissotins suggest that they had shaken his confidence during the bitter debates and pamphleteering on the colonial color question. For theirs had been the principled position, sanctioned by the thought and culture of the age. Against color prejudice and slavery they could cite some of the great texts of the Enlightenment, including not only Rousseau and Raynal, for whom Barnave had no more than a qualified respect, but Montesquieu himself, whom he greatly admired and who was the strongest influence upon him.

On the other hand, the universalist radicalism of the Brissotins showed to less good advantage in the Legislative Assembly (October 1791–September 1792), of which they formed the Left fraction, the group known to history as the Gironde. Undisciplined, intriguing, posturing, orating, they came to concentrate their zeal on the demand for a revolutionary war. In the spring of 1792 the Brissotins were able to gain a position in the ministry by preaching a crusade of liberation for the oppressed peoples

50. Oeuvres II, 62, 68.

against the "crowned tyrants" of Europe (in effect, Austria). To this war the king, Lafayette, and certain Feuillants acceded for their own counterrevolutionary or conservative reasons. Robespierre broke with the Brissotins over the war, dubious of their new allies as well as of the idea of "armed missionaries." Barnave, as we have seen, counseled opportunistic support of the Brissotins *faute de mieux*, but he consistently held that peace on the Continent, especially with Austria, was the keystone of foreign policy. The Brissotins imagined a brief and happy ideological war with Austria, which they argued would consolidate the Revolution in France, stabilize the assignat, and banish the evidences of popular "anarchy" which were beginning to disturb them. They also thought it possible to avoid a naval-commercial war of "interests" with England (perhaps influenced by the interests of the Atlantic ports, especially Bordeaux, where they had many ties). For Barnave, had any war been nationally justifiable at the time, it would have been precisely such a struggle, centering on colonial-commercial objectives, with England.

Politically discredited by the Brissotins on the color question, but in a sense personally vindicated as a result of their political incompetence and their disastrous war, Barnave saw his enemies as mixtures of ambition and idealism, dogmatics and sentimentality, rooted in what he called the "metaphysical and didactic spirit of the age." His fights with the Left in 1791 must have strengthened his skepticism of the eighteenth-century reformist writers generally and enabled him to distance himself intellectually and spiritually from most of his eighteenth-century mentors. For his thought is free not only of their typical universalist intellectual ambitions; it seems to lack that humanistic aspiration which we find in his sources—even in the physiocrats, in Helvétius and Condillac—not to speak of Mably and Raynal, whom he also read. Barnave has, in effect, generalized Hume's and Smith's doubt of "theoretical projectors" to the point where he suspects all schemes of universal improvement and all "systems," whether based on free trade or any other "metaphysical" doctrine. And nowhere do we find any clear enunciation of the moral desirability of democracy, even in the special sense in which he defined it, apart from its objective factuality as one result of modern history. Such silences probably indicate not just mental reservations bred of political disillusionment, but also a fundamental doubt of the easy convergence of what is good with what is true.

Nevertheless, this alienation from the humanism specific to the eighteenth century has a positive, creative side. Barnave turns quite naturally to what he regards as the concrete or material bases, not only of politics and revolution; this is also his approach to the higher aspects of culture. He is interested in the actual social functions of religion and of philosophy itself. And indeed he has assimilated the free thought of his age to the extent that his rejection of religion is coldly realistic and affords no welcome to the surrogate enthusiasm of eighteenth-century philosophizing. Shortly before his trial and execution, when he knew these to be inevitable, he wrote to his sister:

Death is nothing; the more time I have had to look it in the face, the more I have become convinced of this, not only by reflection but by feeling. Today it is my habitual idea and I live with it as calmly and serenely as if I saw it only in the vague distance, as other men do. . . . One indivisible moment . . . beyond which there is no more pain, nor regret, nor memory. . . . [51]

Leaving life he regrets only "friendship and the cultivation of my mind, a habit which has often filled my days in a delightful manner." Utterly secular, apparently an agnostic if not also a materialist, his rapid allusions show him inclined to the positive study of religion in the spirit of Montesquieu. For example, he holds that the "idea" of Calvinism—that is, its ecclesiology and theology—is completely "democratic." Nevertheless, in the sixteenth century the French nobility dominated democratic Calvinism. This paradox was possible, he argues, because the

---

51. Letter of November 13, 1793, translated and quoted by Bradby, *Life* II, 331.

real basis of democracy, commercial property, was then too weak to prevent it—which "demonstrates" the truth of his own historical principles. (See p. 120.) Or, as we might say, Barnave has concretely grasped the difference between the theological-ecclesiastical form and the social function of a religious movement.

His thought moves easily between religious and political phenomena, which for him are not identical, but comparable insofar as they derive from similar social conditions. Barnave was, therefore, far from that twentieth-century sophistication which asserts the incommensurability of the "religious" English revolution and the "political" or "secular" French. Strafford, he holds, had his counterpart in Mounier, the Presbyterians in the Feuillants (*Constitutionnels*), the Independents in the republicans. "Our journals and clubs correspond to their preachers, intermediaries between the leaders and the people."[52] The difference lay between their violent passion of "religious reforms" and our corrosive passion of "philosophizing"—a significant difference, but one of times and modes, not fundamentals, not of social orders.

The discerning penetration which sensed the positivity of religious phenomena extended to Barnave's appraisal of the philosophy of his own century, particularly in its political functions. One might expect a certain sympathy on his part for the philosophical advocates of the *thèse royale* and enlightened despotism, but this was not his feeling. Voltaire he especially deplored: "a superficial and dissipated mind, attached to externals, to the facile; a bad metaphysician; dramas without character, history without bases; a superficial scholar in every area; never a painter of nature."[53] Voltairean enlightenment did attack superstition, but at the price of agreeing to respect the throne. And since the seventeenth century the throne had followed a policy of corruption, sometimes adroitly, sometimes crudely, but consistently aiming to degrade pride and honor,

52. *Oeuvres* II, 69–70.
53. Ibid., IV, 272.

to open prestige to the lowest ambitions, creating a thousand ways to get rich, tending to that kind of equality which makes the security of despotic governments. Barnave refuses to interpret these despotic tendencies as necessary coordinates of the rise of commercial wealth, for as a social institution monarchy has a certain freedom of action and can only be made to function progressively through "national representation," a two-party system, a public budget, and so on. He consistently argued for an energetic central government against all federative (and republican) tendencies—which he saw as closely related in France—but centralization per se held no magic for him and was only meaningful in the context of public institutions and a constitution, not through chicanery and corruption even when these were decorated with bureaucratic philanthropy. And eighteenth-century philosophy, although it would one day help to destroy despotism, had been "prostituted" to the throne's "thoroughgoing system of degradation," which taught the nation only love of gold, pleasure, and frivolous vanity. The corruption of morals is a tendency in large and populous states, and for this reason the government must have strength (*du nerf*), but of a sort which is supplemented not by luxury and avarice, but rather by industry and labor, which "occupy and moralize the people."[54] Philosophy is of doubtful value in this regard, and indeed it only deceives when it attaches to an elite pampered or supported by power, whether of the old or the new regime. Barnave's comments on Condorcet's "Report on Education" (to the Legislative Assembly, April 20-21, 1792) express his general skepticism and disdain of a philanthropic rationalism which, he held, concealed its own ambitions behind its ignorance of history, politics, and institutions. "Public education is to be confided to a body of philosophers or so-called sages, independent of constitutional power . . . dictating doctrine, disposing a large number of employments, many millions of funds." Condorcet's scheme entails a "corporation, a privilege, an aristocracy. . . . The influence of philosophy should come from the liberty of

54. Ibid., II, 6.

the press, not from the delegation of great public powers. Philosophy flourishes in independence and in private life. When science converts itself into public power there arise all the frauds and illusions of charlatanism."[55] Quite apart from the unquestionably political animus behind these criticisms, they are completely consonant with Barnave's interpretation of the origins of the Revolution, and serve to emphasize the difference between him and all those contemporaries and later thinkers, of both Left and Right, who saw in it a great effort to realize philosophy.

The Sense of Modernity and the Idea of the Past

Friedrich Meinecke distinguished in eighteenth-century historiography between Montesquieu's individualizing tendency of thought, which made him a forerunner of Herder and historicism, and the "mechanistic," "external" approach present in Turgot and Condorcet, who belong to the prehistory of nineteenth-century positivism.[56] Despite a number of affinities with the positivist trend, Barnave's basic intellectual and even temperamental disposition bring him much closer to Montesquieu.

To form a good mind which has only the necessary metaphysics, subordinates reasoning to facts, guided by a sensible and enlightened reason; strong in useful imagination, nourished by a spirit of observation [I would put into the hands of the young student] Montesquieu's *Considerations on . . . the Romans.*[57]

In the first place, Barnave follows Montesquieu in renouncing pragmatic historiography—that is, the idea, inherited from classical humanism and still much to be reckoned with in the eighteenth century, that history was "philosophy teaching by example."

55. Ibid., II, 58–59.
56. *Die Entstehung des Historismus* (Munich, 1946), pp. 183–84.
57. *Oeuvres* IV, 255.

From history and from books you may construct a thousand maxims, a thousand examples to admire; but when compared with [things] in the present, they no longer apply. In the eyes of some people the difference will be small, but this difference is everything.[58]

The prepositivists of the eighteenth century, although rejecting pragmatic historiography in the old, simple sense of the dramatic presentation of instructive examples and precedents, shared its underlying conviction of the uniformity of human nature. They held of course that this uniformity—in their view, of the rational and perceptual faculties—would become fully visible only gradually, through the progress of the arts and sciences. Nevertheless, for them rational man was always in principle separable from his historical situation.[59] Now Barnave's skepticism about historical comparison bears not only on traditional humanist, pragmatic historiography's belief in the uniformity of human nature; it involves his dissent from the eighteenth century's optimistic articulation of that belief in the idea of progress.

The prepositivists have this in common with Comte, that they view the record of the arts, of invention, as raw material toward a progressive mental history of mankind. Barnave has no such enterprise: history is not a lawful development based on the constants of human nature. At most he mentions a certain *inquiétude publique* which, however, is variously deployed according to physical and historical circumstances.[60] He does, indeed, speak of "political gravitation," of "the nature of things," "natural advances," "causes," "principles acting with

---

58. Taken from a facsimile of *Cahier* 3, p. 42, of Barnave's papers in the municipal library of Grenoble (U. 5. 216).
59. For an interesting discussion of the Enlightenment's difficulty in holding together the ideas of an unchanging human nature and a progressive humanity, see Ernst Cassirer, *The Philosophy of the Enlightenment*, trans. F. Koelln and J. Pettegrove (Boston, 1964), pp. 216–28.
60. For example, in the fragment "Du progrès des sociétés," as reproduced in Rude, *Barnave*, pp. 67–68.

regularity," and so on;[61] but this language should not be construed (as Montesquieu's analogous language in the first two chapters of the *Spirit of the Laws* should not be) as signifying his subjection of social and historical facts to the laws of a natural science. For Barnave's "causes," "advances," "principles," always refer to the inherently social tendency of population and industry; and the operation of this tendency is not universal, but severely circumscribed by physiographical conditions. Indeed, what may appear to be a geographical determinism actually functions in his presentation to establish the concreteness and historicity of industry and democracy. Thus, Barnave's level of generalization and his organizing concepts are far less abstract than those of the prepositivists, and correspondingly, the facts of commerce and industry as he marshals them are less positive, less brute as it were, in that they are embedded in legal and political systems, self-subsisting and continuing entities. For Barnave, the stages of property, although theoretically linked by the themes of population and work, give rise to integral social systems, each possessing its own unifying principles (excepting always feudalism). His refusal to summarize historical continuity as the mere succession of laboring individuals (or, for that matter, of exchangists, or of accumulators of capital)—his recognition of relative sociopolitical stasis and his strength in particularizing the modern European states— show the influence of Montesquieu and suggest the sense in which Barnave appreciated his *Considerations on . . . the Romans* as well as the *Spirit of the Laws* with its cardinal distinction between republics and monarchies and, generally, Montesquieu's feeling for the totality specific to each society.

Beyond this grasp of what is socially self-subsistent and concrete, although closely related to it, Barnave shares Montesquieu's vision of the uniquely complex nature—psychological, moral, institutional—of the modern world. "A people which has lost its simplicity does not recover it again."[62] The theme

61. "Préambule," or plan of the *Introduction*, ibid., p. 63.
62. *Oeuvres* II, 42 (written during the Convention).

of the complexity and heterogeneity of modern life had become more or less commonplace during the prerevolutionary decades.[63] It seems to have arisen primarily from the study of national literatures and aesthetic taste (which is probably where Barnave first encountered it). But it appeared also in comparative law, ethnography, and notably in the new experience of economic life and the deepening interest in the division of labor and the problems of luxury and poverty. The notion that the present was complicated and derivative played an important part in the eighteenth century's self-awareness. I would suggest also that a consciousness of the heterogeneous and therefore problematic character of modernity nourished historical thinking around the middle of the eighteenth century, and that it helped to form the two contrasting sets of ideas about historical change and the past which were then becoming explicit: (1) the idea that the new widening of experience, understood as an advancement and diffusion of knowledge, tended to make men increasingly sociable and benevolent ("mild" was the eighteenth-century word), and that therefore the unity of mankind and its experience was to be found in its universal *progress;* and (2) the idea that both human experience and action diverged sharply according to time and place, that the modern world was unique and very distant from antiquity, that all nations—ancient and modern—possessed distinctive characters, and that these totalities (which we would call historical individuals) were perhaps comparable, but certainly not on the scale of general amelioration or happiness.

1. It was Adam Smith who made the most serious attempt to subsume economic competition under the larger concept of moral enlightenment and improvement. He developed a kind of sociology based on "sympathy" (as did David Hume), ostensibly to combat the "selfish system" of Hobbes and Mandeville. But sympathy also showed how, in the large and complicated combinations of modern society, it was possible and indeed

---

63. See Henry Vyverberg, *Historical Pessimism in the French Enlightenment* (Cambridge, Mass., 1958).

necessary for individuals, especially of the middling rank, to adjust their passions and actions to what they sympathetically came to perceive as the expectations of others. The enlarging spheres of sympathetic relations gave rise, in turn, to the possibility of an internalized "impartial spectator," enabling people of the widest views to understand the harmony and necessity of a social order based, in the first place, on private motives.[64] Something like Smith's idea, that a knowledge both moral and rational could arise from the experience of complex social relations, played a vital role in Condorcet's belief in a rational altruism; and Smith's "impartial spectator" is obviously close to the intellectualistic content of the idea of progress.

More directly linked to the concept of progress was the effort to unify the phenomena of work, exchange, accumulation, taxation, and so forth through the categories of economically stagnant and progressive societies. From this point of view, the continuity of thought from Hume to Smith and Turgot and finally Condorcet is clear: the emphasis on rational accumulation in a free market tends toward the concept of illimitable progress. Thus the antinomies of the eighteenth-century world— including the intrusion of market relationships into ever widening spheres and the new visibility of wealth and poverty—as well as its chaos of data and experience, found their résumé in the overarching thesis of humanity's endless march toward perfection.

2. On the other hand, thinkers like Montesquieu, Ferguson, and Herder (and earlier, Vico in his own way) tended to emphasize the discontinuity and contrast between a complex and critically unstable modernity and the integral life of ancient, archaic, or primitive societies. From them the old idea of decadence, a persistent temptation for the eighteenth century, received its preromantic or historicizing turn: that is, the view, not that the past began with golden ages intrinsically better

---

64. *Theory of the Moral Sentiments* (1759). I follow G. R. Morrow's ideas about the relationship between this work and *The Wealth of Nations*. (*The Ethical and Economic Theories of Adam Smith* [New York, 1923].)

than the present, but that it contained forms of life and thought which were finished, complete unto themselves, remote from the ordinary experience of moderns, and accessible to them only through a new way of selecting and interrogating sources. This historicizing turn of mind rested, no less than the search for progress, on eighteenth-century realities. For example: Vico's rejection of Cartesian rationalism, which he appears to have generalized by associating reflective periods with the rise of private interests, pleasures, and caprices—i.e., with "a deep solitude of spirit and will," leading to the decline of nations ("the barbarism of reflection"). Or Montesquieu's experience of a disintegrating aristocratic society of orders in which, as he came to theorize, political virtue was irrelevant. Or, finally, Adam Ferguson, who understood (perhaps as early as Adam Smith) the dehumanizing consequences of the modern division of labor, comparing it, not too favorably, with the simpler forms of barbarism.[65] The common element is an awareness of the unexampled multiplicity of conditions, callings, experiences, and finally values imposed by modern life. The thought in this second tendency did not exclude the concept of the unity of mankind, or the comparison of its cultural expressions, or even the ordering of successive stages of social development; but it did exclude the idea of unilinear progress. The unity of history was grasped, not in the external links between civilizations, but rather perhaps through their inner developments, each civilization expressing a particular actualization of a universal principle or set of relations. Thus, the eighteenth-century historicizing tendency—turning Locke's empiricism in a new direction —came to concentrate on the distinctiveness of the various historical and prehistorical societies. And in Greek antiquity especially would be found, not so much the source of European

---

65. *Essay on . . . Civil Society*, pp. 182–83 and passim. For Vico, see T. G. Bergin and M. H. Frisch, trans., *The New Science of Giambattista Vico* (Cornell, 1960), esp. par. 1106. Max Rouché, *La philosophie de l'histoire de Herder* (Paris, 1940), contains a detailed and convenient account of Herder's hostility to enlightened despotism and of his view that commercial and technical progress entailed the fragmentation of life (pp. 60–68).

civilization as a revealing contrast, embodying an irretrievable excellence of life and art.

Now, for all his emphasis on industry, property, and their progressive stages, Barnave's way of thinking comes close to this individualizing, historicizing trend, or at any rate, it gives his ideas a fuller illumination than does the prepositivist elaboration of the idea of progress. His Hellenism, although free of romantic idealization, conveys a negative judgment of modern culture. More broadly, for him the unity of history lies in the possible conclusions of research—economic, legal-political, ethnographic—not in the conclusions of time. Thus his philosophical history stops short of a philosophy of history (in the nineteenth-century sense of that term). Even the progress of the democratic principle, despite its basis in human industry, is not progress generically, for it culminates in an order of large commercial states which is neither inherently pacific nor philanthropic. Human happiness is not history's foregone conclusion. "Nothing is more difficult to determine" than the relative happiness of societies. Are the "contemplative orientals . . . [or] the pastoral and nomadic peoples," spending their lives in "monotonous wanderings . . . more or less happy than our restless (*inquiets*) Europeans?"[66] History is more like a winnowing or harrowing than a cumulative process. The feudal order was distinctly retrograde. Modern times gather up the debris of the ancient world, not its integral achievements, not its natural wisdom and harmony. With us "nothing is indigenous, nothing is primitive, but [rather] the fruit of a thousand different sources, altered and corrupted by one another!" (p. 91)

Barnave shared the current view that the culture of the modern monarchies, with their capitals, salons, and enlarging literary public, was artificial, syncretic. But he seems also to have sensed that this view was itself a component of the culture. That component had been largely shaped by the Rousseauan mode of placing the mechanical progress of civilization in

---

66. *Oeuvres* II, 168.

opposition to the purity of authentic inner sentiments. Recognizing such an opposition, and to a degree accepting Rousseau's construal of it, Barnave nevertheless saw Rousseau as himself part of the problem—the critique of artificiality as itself a source of new artifices in social life. Rousseau "supported sentiment and . . . weakened the progress of egoism, of callousness and moral baseness. . . . [but] also contributed to the confusion of all opinions . . . to the adoption of bizarre and extreme ones." His "new style" widened the emotional setting of sensual love, but he also "made madmen of people who would have been merely fools" (p. 140). Thus artificiality contaminates the literary-moral culture inspired by opposition to it. Barnave probably ascribed Rousseau's wide influence to his highly developed consciousness of the moral problems of the age, yet neither in Rousseau nor in any other eighteenth-century writer does he find a consciousness which transcends these problems, which is truly critical. For him, therefore, the character of the eighteenth century as a present is deeply problematical.

Barnave's way out of this difficulty is, as usual, not abstractly speculative. He does not recommence Rousseau's search for what is "natural." His way is to take the facts of modern morals and consciousness positively, as data of experience. From this viewpoint he seems to sense, at least, the intellectually creative possibilities in the disorders of modernity. A dispassionate appraisal of the eighteenth-century riot of opinions, fads, and enthusiasms might prepare the mind to understand the reality of other forms of thought, strange to moderns, not because of any inherent capriciousness, but because of their historical remoteness. "One may be [so] astonished at the bizarre opinions of the ancient philosophers [as to] attribute the appearance solely to corrupt transmissions. But the equal extravagance of ideas born in our time enables us to deem them possible, and this certitude invites us to investigate the ways in which the human mind goes astray."[67] Of course, "going astray" (*s'égarer*)

---

67. Taken from a facsimile of *Cahier* 3, p. 202, of Barnave's papers in the municipal library of Grenoble (U. 5. 216).

could suggest that this is a didactic, rationalistic judgment of "error" in general. But much closer to his general outlook was the critical attitude toward modern rationalism with its didactic "extravagance," and it would be fairer to say that he uses "our time" comparatively here, in such a way as to invite us to the positive, historical study of various expressions of human thought, errors and all.

The development of historicizing perspectives on past societies out of a critical awareness of eighteenth-century life can, of course, be seen in a much fuller way in writers like Montesquieu and Ferguson; but their sociological depth is, after all, the proper *ambiance* for interpreting Barnave's brief sketches and arguments, which center on the contrast between ancient and modern taste and morals. Montesquieu and Ferguson saw in modern times a basic discontinuity between the motives of individuals and the logic of the institutions that surround them. For them, as for others, Mandeville's "private vices–public benefits" expressed, not the paradox of sociability in general, but something about the texture of contemporary life, a moral dissonance specific to modern societies. Montesquieu argues, for example, that "honor" is the principle of monarchies (that is, the large states of the West as he knows them), not in the sense that they are honorable at home or abroad, but that their social machinery is set in motion by self-regard, and centrally by the nobleman's specific sense of his independence. Thus his truthfulness is honorable, as it connotes his *franchise* and boldness; loyalty, his voluntary attachment to the king's person; morality, his astute conformity to the courtier's code.[68] On the other hand, public spirit and civic virtue are to be found in books about the ancients.

Montesquieu's implicit argument is that the general reason (structure) of modern societies is not morally accessible to their inhabitants, nor need it be so for them to act properly as individuals in those societies. But such interpretations of modernity were critical exposures of its human lacks, for the interpretive

---

68. See *Spirit of the Laws,* Bk. IV, esp. Chap. 2.

procedures were closely tied to the positive delineation of other societies: Montesquieu's account of the "virtue" of the ancient republics, Ferguson's reconstructions of primitive communal life.[69] These treatments showed forms of society where the motives of individual men were communal or political in source and aim, in which the tribesman or citizen was a microcosm of his society, in which his desires and thoughts were continuous with the structure of social conventions around him.

Barnave's remarks on Greek culture, his respect for its unity and integrity, have this kind of relationship to his feeling for his own world. The Greeks were close to nature, he says, and could "paint her directly." They knew nothing of the speculative world of the "artificial, hybrid (*métis*) man without definite origin or character, or the imaginary world of the depraved man, fleeing . . . the sad and disgusting realities that surround him." The ancients lived with things, not merely thoughts. Integrally attached to their world, they did not separate a way of speaking from a way of living. "The man and the writer were not two."[70]

By contrast, the modern man of letters caters to an individual patron, aristocratic or royal, and finally, as literary prestige comes to overshadow noble rank, to an overrefined and narrow public taste. Enlightenment, the "philosophical sect," strips down and purifies language and thought, destroys moral authority, undermines religion, and depletes the imaginative repertory of poetry. Deprived of aliment, enthusiastic temperaments turn to the "new and insipid errors of Mesmer and Saint Martin." But these modish illusions, like all others, are still related to the spirit of the age, which is "metaphysical, didactical."[71]

The modern world was born, as it were, middle-aged, or rather its youth was wasted in "vain imitations" (scholasticism, and perhaps the Renaissance). "When we began [to see] that nature was the true model [i.e., when taste developed], we no longer had

69. *Essay on . . . Civil Society*, pt. II, "Of the History of Rude Nations." For Ferguson's appreciation of Montesquieu, whose ideas were seminal for him, see ibid., pp. 69–70.
70. *Oeuvres* IV, 93–94 ("Of Art among Different Peoples").
71. Ibid., pp. 95–101, 105.

the youth that can perceive and paint her. Genius and taste, which among the Greeks existed together, have been successive among us" (p. 91). Thus modern culture began, not with imagination (heroic ages, epic poetry), but with the erudition of the Renaissance. The courtly heroic French literature of the seventeenth century came too late to achieve classic greatness (although Barnave does honor it as a force in national morale). But in the eighteenth century this courtly imaginative literature gave way to an inferior genre, philosophy, by which he means a worldly kind of erudition, cultivated censoriousness, coldness of heart, criticism, along with precise expression and the appropriation of scientific ideas.[72]

This schema of the stages of modern culture—erudition, imagination, philosophy—is the same as the one propounded by d'Alembert in his "Preliminary Discourse" to the *Encyclopédie* (1751). But d'Alembert was a celebrant of his age, as is obvious in his account of modern philosophy, while Barnave is apparently groping toward a differentiation between the history of commerce and industry, which is progressive per se, and that of general culture, which is not necessarily so.

Thus, the idea of decadence which emerges in Barnave's *Introduction* and in his literary fragments is not the simple negative of eighteenth-century optimism; nor does it derive from the old repertory of humanist formulas: the decay of nature, the cyclical declension of ages, the transitoriness of things human, and so on. Its source was explicitly the actual social world in which the market, labor, opinion, and individual caprice were held to prevail increasingly over the unified sense of life. Barnave's close contemporary Friedrich Schiller, Hellenist and erstwhile fellow traveler of revolution, saw the age in a remarkably similar way. *On the Aesthetic Education of Man* (the letters of the first version were written within months of Barnave's *Introduction*) explains how human rationality and sensual life have been driven apart, now to reveal their fatal antagonism in eighteenth-century culture, society, and the Revolution itself.

72. Ibid., 113–16 ("Of French Taste and Spirit").

Selfishness has established its system in the very bosom of our exquisitely refined society, and we experience all the contagions and all the calamities of community without the accompaniment of communal spirit.

These calamities spring from the actual conditions of modern life where

> enjoyment was separated from labor, means from ends, effort from reward. Eternally chained to only one single little fragment of the whole, Man himself grew to be only a fragment; with the monotonous noise of the wheel he drives everlastingly in his ears, he never develops the harmony of his being, and instead of imprinting humanity upon his nature he becomes merely the imprint of his occupation....[73]

Thus the simplicity and "splendid humanity" of the Greeks put us to shame. The separation of reason and sentiment is "a wound inflicted upon modern humanity ... [by] culture itself." Political reform is therefore problematical, however ardently desired; and now its prospect is especially darkened by revolutionary terror, which reveals how society itself has been riven between the depraved overrefinement of the philosophical public and the brutality of the masses. Nevertheless Schiller, with his somewhat etherealized Jacobinism, could still look forward to an ultimate renewal and reconstitution of social life in and through aesthetic culture and the theater. Barnave, on the other hand, dedicated as he was to the vocation of politics, saw that the public world, at any rate, had already been renovated by commerce and industry, and that the integral life of the sentiments was the chief victim of this renovation.

Seeing this, Barnave is still very far from a romantic idealization of the Greeks or of any other remote people. His historical "principle" and his realism always return his interest to the present. To inquire into the respective advantages of the wealth and poverty of nations would be, he muses, an interesting study. We could compare Athens with Sparta, Carthaginian opulence

---

73. Schiller, *On the Aesthetic Education of Man*, trans. Reginald Snell (New Haven, 1954), pp. 35–40 (fifth and sixth letters).

with Roman virtue, the ideas of Raynal with those of Mably. But for some peoples it is useless to discuss the problem, since it is settled by the facts; and this is "absolutely" our situation. We can no more occupy the situation of the "Anglo-Americans" than a man of forty can return to twenty-five. Nations, like men, do not recover their youth. Take away our wealth, arts, and population, "our mercantile and manufacturing industry," and we will have the debility of infancy without its innocence or happiness. And should this modern desire for renewal take us through "centuries of barbarism," we would emerge nevertheless an "artificial people" (*peuple factice*).[74]

Our world, then, is old, but (*pace* Fontenelle, Turgot, et al.) hardly the wiser for it.

Barnave, Marx, and the Bourgeois Revolution

This pessimism, qualified as it is, tells us something about Barnave's limitations as a revolutionary politician—limitations of temperament, imagination, sympathy—limitations, above all, of situation. The genuinely mythic dimension of the Revolution as a great drama of rebirth escapes him, and he seems to share little in its message of human renewal. A cool and somewhat patrician detachment is evident in his appraisal not only of "philosophy" but of the "people" it proposed to elevate. The people, in the sense of the lowest strata, the voteless and propertyless, are to be treated as minors and their rights protected lest they destroy them.[75] The most turbulent workers of Paris are without property, local loyalty, or political knowledge.[76] In his political memoirs, which fall outside of the *Introduction* proper, Barnave emphasizes the peril and narrowness of the passage through revolution, undoubtedly a reflection of the political impasse in which he found himself by the summer of 1791. The

74. *Oeuvres* II, 200, 201.
75. Ibid., III, 270.
76. Ibid., I, 135–36.

issue as he had come to see it by then was whether to recognize the end of the definitive Revolution or allow it to degenerate into a general subversion of property. In a young people liberty is natural, but among soft and corrupt peoples, liberty depends on careful management, on steering between slavery and license. A certain force is needed in institutions (a constitutional monarch shored up by a strong executive) so that the inheritance of moral corruption in the people can be contained before it overflows like a torrent.[77] In the actual society the property owners, those living by active and useful industry, were little suited to making a revolution, and its undertaking had depended on the support which the nonproprietors gave to a corrupt but talented group of political fortune-seekers.[78] The passage from the old regime to a free and limited monarchy based on "national representation" was dictated by the long-range consequences of the democratic principle, yet the concrete change was not only violent but *unprepared* in the sense that civic spirit was unable to contain popular passion.

Barnave himself was also unprepared for the growing tenacity and organization of the Parisian lower classes—the sans-culottes. In the first place his early rise to leadership of the constitutional Left in 1789–90 precluded any practical political relationship with the Paris poor. But beyond that, his historical concepts stopped short of the full actualities of the Revolution, and indeed of the eighteenth-century economy. For him the "industrious part of the people," the "poor," represent the historic opposition to aristocracy; they are the holders or potential acquirers of *propriété mobilière*. But in fact the landless peasantry, the urban poor, and the pauperized layers beneath them constituted the largest social sector on the eve of the Revolution, and a growing sector. These groups, the actual poor, Barnave left out of account, of politics, and of thought.

On this level, Turgot as rational administrator had conveyed the social realities much better, however complacently, with his

77. Ibid., II, 161–62, 166.
78. Ibid., II, 77–78.

incorporation of subsistence wages, poverty, and sharp economic inequality into an abstract model of production and distribution. Turgot, moreover, was working toward socioeconomic categories of capital and wage labor which would cut across and supersede the distinction between agriculture and industry—at least that relatively crude distinction which was so basic for the physiocrats as well as Barnave, despite his very different perspective on it. The irony is that Turgot as theorist, for all his philanthropic optimism, would have been much better prepared than Barnave to recognize the social tensions within the modern economy.[79]

Barnave, then, as should be clear by now, recognized no basic inequality, certainly no profound social antagonism or conflict, within the modern division of labor—that is, the social world based on private property and liquid capital. In this respect it is idle to measure him against Marx. Much more revealing is the fact that *no* political leader or popular spokesman of the Revolution, including Marat, Robespierre, Saint-Just, and the Hébertistes themselves, admitted a basic conflict between democracy as a political order and commercial-industrial property. The legislator was to assure subsistence or, more radically, provide for the citizen's independence by giving him a small property. Grave inequality was the result, not of the processes of production and exchange per se, but of privilege, monopoly, and chicanery; its cause and cure lay in the political sphere. The aspirations of the Paris sections—organized sansculotterie—did not go beyond this.

The conviction that the economic order as such was intrinsically egalitarian and harmonious united the otherwise

---

79. "In a nation where there is a lively commerce and industry, competition fixes [the wages of labor] at the lowest possible rate." Letter to Hume, March 25, 1767, in *Oeuvres de Turgot* II, 663. See also Turgot's "Réflexions sur la formation et la distribution des richesses" (1766), ibid., pp. 533–601.

The physiocrats themselves, despite their harmonism, did recognize a "necessary" link between expanding social wealth and inequality. See George Weulersse, *Le mouvement physiocratique en France* (Paris, 1910), II, 32–35.

variegated spectrum of revolutionary opinion; and in this connection it indicates something of the strength and consistency of the Revolution's social basis in the middle class of commercial wealth, the bourgeoisie. The conviction was not purely naïve, for the contrary view that the division of labor embodied negative and antagonistic elements had already occurred to Rousseau as the general formula for historical regression, and to Nicolas Linguet in his relentlessly pessimistic exploration of wage "slavery" (*Théorie des lois civiles*, 1767). That such views found little reception in the Revolution (before 1795 and Babeuf, at any rate) suggests that its historic function was the liberation of commercial wealth—that it was, as is widely held today, the social revolution of the bourgeoisie, and not simply a political upheaval. Such of course was Barnave's understanding of it, although instead of bourgeoisie—a term of specialized meaning under the old regime—he spoke of the "industrious (*laborieuse*) part of the people," or of the "poor," or the "commons." He meant by such terms the nonprivileged, especially those living by production and exchange, whose unity of interests required a strong constitutional monarchy and legal safeguards for their commercial wealth. The socially marginal, the underclasses of town and country, would be gradually absorbed as individuals into the "commons" with the destruction of privilege and the advent of legal equality. The idea of the unity of the nonprivileged, classically expressed in Sièyes' pamphlet *What Is the Third Estate?*, became a political commonplace in 1789, fitting quite naturally into the universalistic perspectives of the revolutionaries. And Barnave, who was as we have seen generally dubious of the optimistic universalism of his intellectual mentors and political contemporaries, did share it to the limited but crucial extent of assuming the ultimate unity, within a national framework, of economic life—that is, of the bourgeoisie and the actual poor.

Therefore Barnave's thinking, quite apart from his historical constructions, documents the strength if not the truth of the idea of the unity of the third estate, an idea which was in turn essential to the bourgeoisie in its revolutionary action. And in the needs and actions of the bourgeoisie many modern historians, notably those of a Marxist tendency, see the unity of the French Revolution. This, of course, was Jaurès' interpretation, and to a large degree his continuators, Mathiez and Lefebvre shared it. The idea is most recently exemplified in the work of Albert Soboul, who concludes that even the radical popular movement of the sansculotterie, his special study, was antiaristocratic in ideology and bourgeois in its historical function.[80]

This is not the place to explore the modern scholarly question of the social character of the French Revolution, and of the objective validity of Barnave's historical generalizations. However, it should be pointed out that the general thesis of the French Revolution as a social movement expressing the coming into its own of the bourgeoisie has been recently challenged by Alfred Cobban in *The Social Interpretation of the French Revolution*. In the course of an exceedingly complex argument and a multitude of conclusions, Cobban makes two points which may be profitably examined with Barnave's role and ideas in mind.

One of Cobban's main arguments is that the bourgeoisie, in either the narrow or broad meaning of the term, played no significant part in the political revolution; that in the broad sense of people connected with commercial property it was profoundly and manifoldly divided; and that the Revolution was made by lawyers and officials (who dominated the Constituent Assembly) to the ultimate benefit of conservative landownership. Therefore, says Cobban, the Revolution was a political rearrangement or reconsolidation and not a social movement at all.[81] The argument assumes that the political action of a social

---

80. *The Parisian Sans-Culottes and the French Revolution, 1793–94* (Oxford, 1964), an abridgement of *Les sans-culottes parisiens en l'An II* (Paris, 1958).
81. Alfred Cobban, *The Social Interpretation of the French Revolution* (Cambridge, Eng., 1965), ch. VI, "Who were the Revolutionary Bourgeois?" and ch. VIII, "A Bourgeoisie of Landowners."
A much more serious case against the interpretive tradition of a bourgeois revolution based on the historic growth of commercial property—the tradition which Barnave anticipates—has been made by George V. Taylor, "Noncapitalist Wealth and the Origins of the French Revolution," *American Historical Re-*

class must derive from its palpable, absolute unity (in supposing the possibility of such a unity Cobban may be thinking of a caste or order), and that this action must be the work of clearly identifiable members of that class. But it seems clear that Barnave, although a lawyer with connections in the nobility and officialdom, not only spoke for the bourgeoisie of commercial wealth (as did his liberal-aristocratic friends in the Constituent Assembly), but himself recognized the political passivity and divisiveness of the class per se. He understood quite well that the possessors of commercial wealth were generally incapable of political initiative and cohesion, even in their own defense. But unlike Cobban, who thinks such data establish the political nullity of the bourgeosie as a whole, Barnave, *en grand bourgeois,* viewed the disabilities of the propertied as political problems and set about dealing with them from the tribune of the assembly, in its committees, in his correspondence, in the Jacobin and later the Feuillant clubs,[82] and last but not least, in his part in founding the *Logographe,* a journal of serious political reportage intended for sound men of wealth. Certainly he would have had no difficulty in admitting what has since become a commonplace in the history of parliamentary institutions: that aristocratic "notables," and later lawyers, have provided most of the political cement of the bourgeoisie. Moreover, his way of thinking would have prepared him to see what Cobban

---

view, LXXII, no. 2 (January 1967), 469–496. Taylor argues for a category of "proprietary" wealth (titled landholdings, offices, etc.) in which the upper Third Estate (as well as the nobility) was strongly represented. He also maintains that commercial wealth of a capitalist character was deeply entwined in the fiscal structure of the old regime, that many capitalist enterprises were controlled by nobles and that, in any event, such enterprises were not typical of bourgeois fortunes. Unfortunately, since the scope of this important article is nothing less than the whole historiography of the social origins of the Revolution, it cannot be adequately discussed within the framework of this treatment of Barnave's opinions and interpretations.

82. In his memoir-narrative of the Constituent Assembly he would write that apart from the leaders, who were "ardent spirits . . . journalists or pamphleteers," the members of the Jacobins were "for the most part of the same mind [as the Feuillants], peaceful men, property owners." *Oeuvres* I, 138.

and many other modern critics cannot, namely, that such questions as the unity, consciousness, revolutionary potential, and even the very existence of a social class cannot be settled by merely examining a cross section of the flux of social development; that the modern concept of social class is intrinsically historical; and that therefore such questions must be posed historically and comparatively, investigated over sufficient spans of time.

Another of Cobban's arguments, and seemingly one of the weightiest in his whole case against the social interpretation of the French Revolution, rests on the claim, in itself quite valid, that French economic life declined during the Revolution and the postrevolutionary decades, not to regain its prerevolutionary vigor until the 1820's.[83] Out of the legal regime of modern private property and laissez-faire came, not the liberation of commerce and the development of large-scale industry, but a conservatizing triumph of landowners, large and small. These facts are adduced to demonstrate that, since the Revolution was not bourgeois in its function or effects, it was not bourgeois at all. But what Cobban never mentions—and Barnave never forgot —is the Revolution's specific national framework and the international rivalries thereto consequent. The Revolution was a critical juncture in the history of France, not purely and simply because it destroyed the old regime, but because it opened the final phase, the climacteric, of a century-long struggle with England for the wealth of the Caribbean, of India, and indeed for the commerce of Europe and the world. Had Napoleon been able to cross the English Channel, who can doubt that the social energies mobilized by the Revolution would have won for the French bourgeoisie not only the plunder of the Continent, but preeminence in world trade and large-scale manufacture, and that the French economy would have become classically bourgeois? On the other hand, can the long-term economic stagnation and conservatism to which Cobban alludes be understood

---

83. Cobban, *Social Interpretation*, ch. VII, "Economic Consequences of the Revolution."

INTRODUCTION: AS PHILOSOPHICAL HISTORIAN 63

without the defeat of Napoleon and the resulting constriction of the French bourgeoisie's field of exploitation? Well before the French revolutionary armies deepened the already existing French threat to English commerce, Barnave was fully aware of the stakes in the rivalry with England. He had sharply criticized the liberalization of trade across the Channel in the Eden treaty of 1786. We know his advocacy of colonies and navies, his strong feeling for national unity, his close attentiveness to the various national articulations of his "principle" in modern Europe. His thought presages the emergence of the nation-state as the enduring political form of the domination of the European bourgeoisie, for all its cosmopolitanism real or imagined.

Contemporary investigations show how limited was the impact of French Jacobinizing and republican ideologies, even in western Europe during the revolutionary era.[84] Robespierre's coldness to the idea of liberating oppressed foreign peoples by armed missionaries shows the bedrock of political realism beneath the

84. In his *Age of the Democratic Revolution: The Challenge* (Princeton, 1959), R. R. Palmer writes that "It is true . . . that persons of revolutionary persuasion were able to install revolutionary regimes only where they could receive help from the French Republican army" (p. 7). To be sure, Palmer is arguing the general thesis that the French Revolution was part of a larger revolution in "Western" or "Atlantic" civilization between 1760 and 1800, and he would doubtless consider the question of the "impact" of the French Revolution on Europe as badly posed, since "persons of revolutionary persuasion" were eager to welcome it. According to Palmer, these sympathizers expressed a European and American protest against aristocratic privilege and closed societies, a protest which both preceded and surrounded the French upheaval. Jacques Godechot, *La Grande Nation* (Paris, 1956), 2 vols., holds the same general position. These two wide-ranging works give more weight to political changes than to specific social transformations, a result of their premises no less than their methods. In extending the Revolution beyond its national framework they deemphasize the paradigmatic historical importance of the social struggles within the French Revolution. Barnave's ideas cannot be properly assimilated to the Godechot-Palmer interpretation, for while he speaks of a "European revolution" this is clearly in the sense of a secular—and nationally differentiated—advance of the "industrious class" rather than of an actual European or Atlantic democratic movement or front. Barnave, whose conservative *political* views do fall within Palmer's (very broad) understanding of eighteenth-century "democracy" (*Age of . . . Revolution*, p. 4), nevertheless saw no difficulty for revolutionary France in coming into regular relations with "unregenerated" states such as Austria.

fanaticism of virtue—shows his very bourgeois awareness of the national limits of revolutionary renewal. Barnave exemplifies the revolutionary bourgeoisie in a simpler way, and although his sense of the national framework of the Revolution was clearer than Robespierre's, it was not essentially different.

Barnave, therefore, is a classic embodiment of bourgeois political culture in its heroic period. One of the central figures in the struggles and reconstructive efforts of the early Revolution, he was kept by his far from sentimental political education as well as his own personal temper from any doctrinaire adhesion to the leading "general ideas" of his age—not only what was called philanthropy but "philosophical economics" as well. His failure to perceive any basic conflict within the modern division of labor was a limitation imposed not by theory but by political experience. In any event, the unity and democracy which Barnave professed to see within the realm of commerce and industry did not, as we have seen, stem from any need on his part to magnify the cultural superiority or unity of the triumphant bourgeoisie. Thus, despite a certain formal similarity of conclusions between Barnave and his ostensible heirs, the liberals of the July monarchy, he shows none of their harsh and complacent Philistinism, their self-identification with "civilization," fed by their hidden fear and shame in the face of the working class—the *"classe laborieuse et dangereuse"*—and what they called the "social question." Even Thierry and Guizot, who were confident enough to examine the historical credentials of the third estate, interpreted its rise and its Revolution as inherently conservative and defensive assertions of rights against the incursions of aristocracy or absolutism. Barnave on the other hand, saw the rise of the "poor," the producers, as a process involving centralized states, transformed legal systems, armies, international economic rivalries, and, underlying all of these, the development of the mechanical arts and urban industry. Barnave's assumption of the connectedness of social conditions and public events, his candid combination of what was socially lowest and highest, led Jaurès to incorporate his ideas in the *Histoire socialiste*. This attentiveness to the material bases of society links him to the tradition of the great political economists of the eighteenth century, and thus finally, to the prehistory of Marxism.

It would appear that Marx himself did not know Barnave's writings.[85] Had he read them, we may guess that he would have been drawn to Barnave's materialism, his skeptical turn of mind, his taste for research, his Hellenism, his consistently antimetaphysical attitude. And more generally, insofar as Barnave's philosophical history embodies a reasoned meditation on man's development from a viewpoint itself understood as epochal in that development, Marx doubtless would have read the *Introduction* as an anticipation of his own historical materialism.

It is only within this tradition of the philosophical history of civil society that the really significant difference of thought emerges. A clue to that difference lies in the fact that Marx was deeply interested in the *process* of revolution itself—his whole *oeuvre* may be said to revolve around a theory of revolutionary action—whereas Barnave thought of the French Revolution, for all the strength of its causal determination, as an "explosion," a perilous interlude, endangered by ambitious "journalists," safeguarded by responsible leaders like himself. In other words, Barnave not only did not, but probably could not very well have explained his own career as revolutionary—not, that is, in accordance with his own historical ideas (though this failing is hardly unusual among revolutionists).

But these different understandings of revolution have to do

---

85. Marx was never hesitant in acknowledging his sources, but there is no reference to Barnave in any of his works. Still, it is curious that this gargantuan devourer of books should have missed the *Oeuvres*, which were published in Paris shortly before his arrival. The fact that the editor, Bérenger de la Drôme, was a peer of conservative tendency (as is apparent in his moralizing introduction) may have led Marx to believe that Barnave's was but one of a number of apologetic political memoirs by old "Constituents." Moreover, Marx's interest in the Revolution was concentrated on the insurrectionary Commune of 1792 and on the Convention. See Jean Bruhat, "La Révolution française et la formation de la pensée de Marx," Annales historiques de la Révolution française, vol. XXXVIII, no. 184 (April-June 1966), pp. 125–70.

with the ways in which Barnave and Marx conceived the relationship between civil society and the political order. Both held that modern society was inherently subject to disequilibrating forces. Barnave saw such forces behind "luxury," which, like the advanced thinkers of the period, he regarded as one *effect* of developed commerce and industry on social morale (rather than as the *cause* of individual and social corruption). Nevertheless, it was with such effects that political culture had to deal. For all practical purposes, Barnave took the social economy as *given*. He therefore grasped the social problem from the point of view of the legislator, as had, broadly speaking, Montesquieu himself. Marx, of course, was more centrally and immediately concerned with the disequilibrating forces in modern society, which he saw taking definitive form in the struggle of industrial proletariat and bourgeoisie. Barnave speaks of softness, corruption, as a political problem; Marx, of a general crisis which engulfs all humanity, including every observer, every "authoritative" position, and especially the legislator's, be it even furnished with political-economic knowledge. For the only knowledge that truly comprehends the crisis of modern society is that which gives mastery through its continuity with revolutionary practice.

In Barnave's view, the political function was crucial in modern society, not as revolutionary action or conservative defense, but as a comprehensive, coordinating activity based on contemporary knowledge of political economy, history, the possibilities of public administration. Knowledge of these kinds enabled the politician to grasp the critical problem: the tendency of commerce and industry to evoke the countertendency of luxury, egoism, and loss of civic spirit. And this problem or conflict was a distinctive result of modern history, of democracy. It might appear from certain of Barnave's notes that he identified luxury with a decaying aristocracy, i.e., with a disappearing past; and this is to an extent the case. However, even in large monarchical states, with an old nobility, where wealthy merchants finally come to adopt aristocratic modes of ostentation, they do so, he seems to think, because of needs of their own which are not satisfied by the ethics of industry. Moreover, in small republics, where there is no rooted nobility, the vanguard of mercantile wealth inevitably elevates itself to new honors above the democracy of work and thrift. Somehow, then, modern social morale is not the simple sum of the moral tendencies of industrious individuals as such. "The morals of a commercial nation are not completely those of merchants. The merchant is thrifty; general morals are prodigal" (Appendix, 9). And this discontinuity exists, not simply because of the surviving strength and attractive power of aristocracy, but rather—insofar as we may elaborate Barnave's thinking —because within the social order of democracy itself there is some latent disharmony which prevents the industrious class of the people from building up, out of its ordinary experience, its own coherent cultural world. It is as if the tension and conflict which Barnave refused to see within the modern division of labor reappears in what is for him the more comprehensive sphere of politics, as a disorder of customs and morals (*moeurs*), of taste and sensibility. Developed national commerce juxtaposes industry and opulence, thrift and prodigality, abstention and luxury, the practical unity of the market and the state on the one hand and the moral isolation of egoistic purposes on the other. Thus modern life, in contrast to the Greek world, is not only derivative in its cultural origins, but witness, in its common activity, to a persistent threat to the sense of community and the wholeness of experience. The fragmentation of experience can be recognized in the study of history and of national literatures. Its partial overcoming, or better, arrest, depends on political life—indeed on political culture.

Now this vision of fragmentation was given a much more dynamic and dramatic quality by Marx, and this resulted from his way of enlarging the notion of the division of labor to embrace the higher culture and politics. Economic competition progressively dissolves all idyllic bonds and conventions, the system of estates, local and national loyalties, and finally, the moral cohesion of the bourgeoisie itself. In modern society, says Marx, communities of sentiment and even of interest tend to lose their substance, becoming instead fantastic projections of a miserable human condition, surrogates for the reality of the world market. The state itself comes to be seen as a phantom community, gradually disclosing its true character as the "political committee" of the bourgeoisie, of naked force. But for Barnave the political function of the modern state is no mere reflex of social conditions. It is an enduring and necessary counterpart of the democracy of the industrious. In constitutional monarchy lies the remedy of the general moral disorders evoked, despite themselves, by commerce and industry. The problem, notes Barnave, is

> to obtain from commerce and the arts their useful effects—population, work, activity, national power, easy circumstances in all classes—[but] to separate their vicious effects: narrow and exclusive avarice, venality, corruption of morals, indolent and ostentatious luxury, [as well as] the inequality of wealth which produces aristocracy in republics, [and] that degradation of soul which ends by weakening the source of wealth in attacking the political power of the nation.[86]

The conflict of industry and luxury, however grave, remains for Barnave the "great political problem," "perhaps the most important subject of modern policy *(politique moderne)*."[87] The task of the legislator, therefore, involves the reconciliation of the antinomies of civil society. His role is seen as one of not simply giving the laws, but building a political culture which includes, within the framework of constitutional monarchy and a well-organized public administration, a disciplined national army, political parties, a free press, and the other institutions of "opinion" which strengthen social morale.

Hegel's *Philosophy of Right* (1821) expressed a similar point of view, in a much more systematic and developed way, to be sure: that the historical resolution of the besetting conflicts of modern life, moral as well as economic, lay in the political sphere, in a monarchy elevated above the centrifugal particularities of civil society (supported, as the more conservative Hegel

---

86. Taken from a facsimile of *Cahier* 2, p. 117, of Barnave's papers in the municipal library of Grenoble (U. 5. 216).
87. "Du progrès des sociétés," Rude, *Barnave*, p. 68.

INTRODUCTION: AS PHILOSOPHICAL HISTORIAN   69

saw it, by a "universal class"—a rational bureaucracy—and vocational corporations). These viewpoints question, in effect, the "economic" version of an autonomous, self-regulating civil society, but they do not go so far as to imply that the political order exhausts the meaning of social life (in the manner of the natural-law absolutists). Rather, they assume a basic heteronomy, within particular states, of the political and social spheres. This assumption derives from Montesquieu and his distinction between the spirit of a people (or "principle" of society) and the "nature" (form) of its government—that is, between civil society and political power. The distinction became a cardinal one in eighteenth-century thought, and it is no surprise to find that for Barnave the datum of organized political power is not obliterated by the profound current of human industry, or that the rivalry and conflict of powerful states remain for him ineluctable limits to the progress of industry and opinion.

In these respects nineteenth-century thought, whether in advanced forms of liberalism or in socialism, registered an important change: the political order tends to lose its categorical weight and autonomy and is seen as the sphere of the pragmatic and provisional. As for Marx, his derivation of the state from the concept of civil society reflected the actuality of "machinofacture" and its world-shaking successes, as well as the resultant working-class movement. These developments, together with the general weakening of political legitimacy in the wake of the French Revolution, portended for him the possibility of human self-government without the state's coercive apparatus. Marx's view of the irresistible gigantism of modern industry as a social process—of the world-historical dimensions of modern social development—influenced his reconstruction of the "natural history" of civil society in stages or forms which he derived from specific *social* modes of production. For Marx, the form of social cooperation, the division of labor, is logically if not historically prior to forms of property and coercion. The case is somewhat different for Barnave, in whose time large-scale industry had hardly appeared in France. The stages of society—hunting, pastoral, agricultural, commercial-industrial—have in common, indeed seem to be derived from, man's relations to various kinds of *things,* his "possessions." They are, above all, property forms, not understood as specific productive modes, but rather as each a system, aristocratic or democratic, of domination. Barnave was primarily interested in the conflict between landed and "movable" property, and the abstractness of this conflict of forms is apparent in his failure to differentiate within the latter between commercial and industrial property. What he calls generically commercial property (*propriété mobilière*) is understood to underlie the unity of the "poor," the "industrious class," and its defense calls for constitutional monarchy. For Barnave it is finally not the critical dynamism of social cooperation, but its political integration that remains the most reliable guide to modern history.

Barnave, then, was a revolutionary of 1789, not 1848, adequate to his age, interpreting his world by the lights of his time. But just as the French Revolution carried within itself the seeds of nineteenth-century radical democracy, so the figure of this revolutionary of 1789 evokes something of the coming age. In spite of, or perhaps together with, his intellectual sobriety, his life conveys a passionate seriousness of youth, new to the eighteenth century, sensed perhaps by Stendhal when he culled from the manuscripts of this other Grenoblois a number of epigraphs for *The Red and the Black*. The illusions of which Barnave was so impatient were not those of youth, but of fashion, philosophizing, senescence. He inclined towards materialism, but the doctrine did not persuade him, as was its frequent tendency in the eighteenth century, that "after all" reality constituted a fixed and finished order of things, exemplary of a juste milieu, of mature wisdom. (His outlook recalls Diderot's in this.) He seems to have believed rather that the notion of the real world was acutely restricted by the illusions of the age, that behind these lay a thesaurus of possibilities, opportunities, and surprises beyond the power of systems and fantasies to comprehend.

Within the limits of the natural and the possible, reality has a richness, singularities, varieties, excesses, well beyond that which timid and sterile speculation would dare or know how to constitute (*composer*). Nature is richer than fiction.[88]

It may be that this feeling for the openness of things, strengthened by his native self-possession and sense of personal honor, kept Barnave from vindictiveness and from reaction, and held him to the Revolution. For he seems to have continued to support it in the larger sense—the patriotic cause, even the mistaken war—despite his disgrace, obscurity, and imprisonment, refusing what would have been an easy emigration, or later an easy escape. Publicly he was identified with the then impossible position of constitutional monarchy, a position he made no attempt to renounce; but privately, and for his own edification, he developed historically the "principle" of democracy, learning also in his isolation to accept the nearing prospect of his own trial and death with a degree of equanimity. It is interesting to speculate as to what this political intellectual made of his coming death. He had been thrust aside by the Revolution's own democracy, for which he doubtless felt a personal disdain. Nevertheless, he does not try to give this attitude an ontological status, but instead, thinks "democracy" into an explanation of the course of modern history and the outbreak of the Revolution. Can it be, further, that Barnave sensed, in the continuing development of the Revolution, that democracy had *necessarily* gone beyond constitutional monarchy, and that the latter was after all a transient, ephemeral form—in that sense "provisional"? But if he did perhaps become aware in this way of the possibility that history had rejected his program, he was not one to consider his own political actions as "provisional," that is, as retrospectively justifiable by appeal to circumstances and contingencies, and separable from their historical entailments. In other words, he would not easily have forgotten his own early revolutionism.

88. *Oeuvres* III, 133.

Had he not welcomed the popular movements of 1788 and 1789 and participated in their illegalities? When, in July 1789, the Intendant of Paris, Berthier, was butchered by a revolutionary mob, had he not, in the National Assembly, uttered the chilling words "was that blood, then, so pure?" True, his personal motives he doubtless considered superior to those of his enemies on the Left—"insects thriving in putrefaction," as he put it. But were not the acts of these enemies and their Montagnard successors, who were now revolutionizing the revolution he had begun, consequences in a political sense of his own acts? With respect, then, to human actions (as distinguished from conscious intentions), could the "sound" revolution be nicely dissevered from the second, republican revolution? Barnave's ability to recognize the continuity of the two revolutions may have been enhanced by the downfall, in May-June 1793, of the Brissotins, whom he held in contempt, and the resulting triumph of the Montagnards, whom he professed to see as "infinitely less hypocritical," as enemies of his Brissotin enemies, and more positively as defenders, like himself, of national unity.[89] We do not know if he allowed such judgments to become truly reflexive, so as to involve a reevaluation of the significance of his own political course; but if he did, we can understand much better the unity of his intellectual and political life. Then, Barnave's historical meditation on democracy, together with his acceptance of the Republic's legality, and thus of his own death, would have been

---

89. *Oeuvres* II, 327 (letter to Alquier, a friendly deputy, January 1793); and Barnave's defense before the Revolutionary Tribunal, ibid., 363, 380–81, 389. Of course, his statements in the latter document must be taken with a certain caution, not only because they come to us through the notes of his counsel, but because of his natural interest in gaining the sympathy of the sans-culotte court.

It is of interest to compare his portraits of Brissot and Robespierre, reproduced in the same volume. The former he dismisses as a "facile intelligence," sustained by "malice," who wanted to introduce a "kind of quakerism, without his having the [necessary] warmth of spirit, nor the virtues of a sectary." Robespierre Barnave likes no better, but "those who will write the history of our revolution cannot neglect to present this singular man . . . always guided by concentrated, inner passions. . . ." Ibid., 66–68.

acts affirming the responsibility for his own life as a political being. It is difficult, at any rate, to imagine Barnave—that rather arrogant but penetrating exposer of illusions—settling for a self-justification short of such a one—one which implied, moreover, a certain conception of revolutionary honor. The era of secular social struggles which opened with the French Revolution has discovered no other.

Be that as it may, it is clear that Barnave sought to appropriate, not to expunge or spiritualize his political experience. He wrote of the "immense space traversed in three years. . . . What mind in individuals, what courage in the masses, but how little firmness of character, calm force and above all real virtue. . . ." Yet on reflection he was convinced that, whatever happened, "we cannot cease to be free and . . . the principal evils which we have destroyed will never appear again." Also strong is the note of disillusionment: "Now that I have returned home again I have asked myself whether I might just as well never have left it."[90] But one may be reasonably sure that this disillusionment arose, not from the disappointments of philosophy, or what would conventionally be called the idealism of youth, but rather from the ephemeral character of his own power and influence. Such disillusionment reinforced his strong familial affections and also, what was probably continuous with them, his taste for thought and study. From 1792–93 may date some of his curious notes on diet, hygiene, and the physical humors in relation to mental activity; possibly also some of his rather fine literary judgments. But clearly his absorbing study lay in his own experience of revolution, and this not in the personal or private sense of memoir or even philosophizing reflection, but as politics in its larger meaning, an experience the full dimensions of which he thought to recover in history.

Thus, the eighteenth century's enterprise of philosophical history draws to a close with this effort of one of the leading

90. Quoted from Barnave's notes, ca. March 1792, in the Archives nationales (W. 15. *registre* ii. I), by Bradby, *Life* II, 304.

revolutionaries to comprehend historically what was, after all, his own life. In this respect Barnave's *Introduction* not only points forward to historical materialism, but carries the intimation of a larger and more persistent question—that of the nature of revolutionary action.

Antoine-Pierre-Joseph-Marie Barnave

INTRODUCTION TO THE FRENCH REVOLUTION

Note on the Translation

In this translation (and in the following Appendix) all interpolations are given in brackets. The full title was originally supplied by Bérenger in his *Oeuvres de Barnave* (see p. 1, n. 1), as were many of the chapter heads. I follow him in most of the latter. The interpolations in the text are mainly mine, although I have been guided by Rude's reconstructions in some of them (see, again, the footnote just cited).

In the original manuscript Barnave marked a number of breaks or gaps in his presentation, usually by dashes. Where these breaks are not supplied by the bracketed interpolations I have indicated them by suspension points.

Chapter I

[*General Point of View*]

We shall try in vain to form a correct idea of the great revolution which has just convulsed France if we consider it in isolation, detaching it from the history of the great states that surround us and of the centuries that have preceded our own. In order to judge its nature and assign its true causes, we must take a longer view and discern the position we occupy in a larger system. It is in contemplating the general movement which has determined the successive changes of form of European governments from feudalism to our time that we perceive clearly the point at which we have arrived and the general causes that have led us to it.

Certainly, revolutions of governments, like all natural phenomena which depend on the passions and will of man, cannot be subjected to those fixed, calculable laws which apply to the movements of inanimate matter. However, among the multitude of causes whose combined influence produces political events, there are some which are so intimately connected with the nature of things—whose regular and constant action dominates so clearly over accidental causes—that after a certain period of time they almost inevitably produce their effect. Almost always it is such elements that change the face of nations. All minor events are caught up in their general results. They prepare the great epochs of history, while the secondary causes to which [these epochs] are almost always attributed only serve to occasion them.

Chapter II

[*That Which Produces the Form of Governments*]

The will of man does not make laws: it has little or no effect on the form of governments. It is the nature of things—the social era at which the people have arrived, the land which they inhabit, their wealth, their needs, their habits, their customs—that distributes power; and this according to time and place: to one, to several, to all, dividing it in various proportions. Those who are in possession of power by the nature of things establish laws in order to exercise it and keep it in their hands. Thus empires are organized and constituted. Gradually the advances of the social state create new sources of power, weaken the old ones, and change the balance of forces. Then the old laws cannot long endure. Since new authorities have appeared in fact, new laws must be established to give these authorities activity within a definite system. So governments change form, sometimes by a slow, imperceptible development and sometimes by violent shocks.

Among the different bases on which power can be established, there are three principal ones whose influence dominates all others and which are especially important to study. These are: (1) armed force, military command; (2) property; (3) the dominance of public opinion. These are the natural powers which, sometimes united, sometimes opposed [constitute governments].

Chapter III

[*General Application of These Ideas from Feudal Government to the Present*]

I shall apply these ideas to the history of European political institutions from feudal government to the present. My observations are not based on historical subtleties, but on universally recognized facts. They may be susceptible to many objections in detail, but I believe the general system has a solid truth. Let us sketch a rapid outline of the most natural distribution of power in the various stages of a society which passes successively through all the developments of population and industry. Although the ideas that can be given in a few pages on such an extensive subject are necessarily imprecise, they may nevertheless throw much light on what I have to say about the succession of political forms in the governments of Europe.

In the earliest ages of society man, living by hunting, scarcely knows the concept of property. His bow, his arrows, the game he has killed, the skins that serve to cover him, constitute almost all his wealth. All the land is common to all. At that period political institutions, if they exist at all, cannot have property as a basis; democracy at this stage is nothing but natural independence and equality. The necessity of a war chief provides the first elements of monarchy. The authority of knowledge, always greater when the mass of men is more ignorant, gives birth to the first aristocracy, that of old men, priests, soothsayers, healers—the origin of brahmins, druids, augurs—in a word, of all aristocracy founded on knowledge, which everywhere precedes that of arms and of wealth, and which, from the very beginning of societies, invariably acquires great power by some real services supported by a great repertory of deception.

When the growth of population makes man feel the need of a less precarious and more abundant subsistence he binds himself to more assiduous efforts: he tames animals, raises herds, and a pastoral people develops. At this time property begins to influence institutions. The man attached to the care of his herds no longer has all the independence of the hunter. Poor and rich cease to be equals, and natural democracy has already disappeared. The necessity of defending properties requires that more energy be given to military and civil authority. Those disposing it gain wealth by power, and [in turn] through wealth aggrandize power and fix it in their hands. Finally, in that stage of societies there can exist combinations where aristocratic or monarchical power becomes vastly extended. The example of several Asiatic regions proves it, but to develop these is not part of my subject.

Finally, the needs of the population constantly increasing, man is obliged to seek his nourishment in the bosom of the earth. He ceases to be a wanderer and becomes a cultivator. Sacrificing the rest of his independence, he ties himself, so to speak, to the land and acquires the necessity of habitual labor. At that time the land is divided among individuals; property no longer includes only the herds that cover the earth, but the earth itself. Nothing is held in common: soon the fields, forests, and even streams become property; and this right, steadily extended, influences the distribution of power more and more strongly.

It would seem that the extreme simplicity of a purely agricultural people should accord with democracy. However, a deeper analysis, and above all history, prove that the moment when a people arrive at the cultivation of the land, and do not yet possess the manufacturing and commercial skill that follows upon it, is the period of social organization in which aristocratic power acquires the greatest strength. At this time it almost always dominates and subjugates the democratic and monarchical influence.

Rarely and perhaps never does it happen that the first distribution of lands is made with any equality.

If the division is carried out on virgin land and possession is by the simple right of occupation—the people usually possessing some political institutions, some established powers at the time they have achieved this third stage of society—the distribution of lands will be made according to the rank, power, and size of herds which each enjoys. What would the poor and the weak man do with a vast field which he cannot clear? He will voluntarily confine himself to bare necessity, while a tribal chief will occupy the whole area he can cover with his herds and cultivate with his servants and slaves; for it is a humiliating circumstance of the history of societies that property in men has almost always preceded that in land, [just] as the custom of taking slaves in war has preceded the degree of population that made tillage and labor a necessity.

When possession of the land is the fruit of conquest, the inequality of distribution will be even greater as a result of the prevailing customs of the epoch. Conquest almost always despoils the vanquished of the greater part of their goods and often reduces them to slavery. Among the victors it enriches hardly anyone but the chiefs, [while] the soldier finds in his share scarcely enough to support for a short time his arrogant indolence.

Thus, from the first moment that a people cultivate the land, it is held in very unequal portions. But [even] when there exists a certain initial equality, however little this is undermined by the natural course of things, the inequality of possessions soon becomes extreme. It is a definite principle that where the only revenue is that of land, the big holdings gradually engulf the small ones; while where there exists a revenue from commerce and industry, the labor of the poor gradually succeeds in winning for them a portion of the lands of the rich.

If there exists no product but that of the soil, he who possesses only a small portion will often be reduced, either by his negligence or the inclemency of the seasons, to a lack of necessities. Then he borrows from the rich man, who, lending each year a small portion of his savings, soon succeeds in taking over [the borrower's] field. The more the rich man impoverishes the poor, the more he takes him into dependence: he makes it seem a favor to feed him while making him cultivate his lands and including him among his servants; and if the law allows, he will buy his very liberty.

The man attached to the cultivation of the soil has sacrificed all natural independence. He is bound to the soil because it enables him to live. The land no longer offers refuge or subsistence to one who neither makes nor possesses anything.

The poor cultivator, scattered over the countryside, at the mercy of his needs, is even poorer because of the nature of his work, which separates and isolates him. It is the coming together of men in towns that enables the weak, through their numbers, to resist the influence of the powerful. The development of the [mechanical] arts is what makes these aggregates numerous and stable.

Finally, in that stage of society the poor man is no less subjugated by his ignorance, having lost the natural sagacity, the boldness of imagination, that characterize man wandering in the forests—those customs and anxious maxims of wisdom which are the fruit of the contemplative life of pastoral peoples. He has not yet acquired the knowledge and confidence of thought which wealth and the progress of the [mechanical] arts disseminate in all classes of society. Habitually solitary, absorbed by continual and unvaried labor, he offers an example of the lowest level to which human nature can fall. All superstitions have the power to enslave him.

Thus some inhabitants easily acquire over the multitude the triple empire of wealth, force, and education, and fix in their hands the government of the state, justice, military command, the priesthood.

In that epoch aristocratic power ordinarily grows in proportion to the decrease of monarchical power.

As long as tribes live by hunting or by means of herds wandering over the land in endless migrations, often disputing territory with other tribes, often combining the resource of brigandage with their customary occupations, and ceaselessly making war from necessity or from idleness, they almost always have need of a general or a chief. But in yielding to the cultivation of the land they become stationary; their existence, unstable and violent at first, gradually becomes more tranquil; and monarchical power decays because it ceases to be useful and because the aristocracy which then arises disputes and soon seizes the preeminence.

In this state of affairs the existence of great empires is difficult. If they are established as a result of political events, they can hardly endure except in a federative form. Since there is no commerce, the parts are not united by their needs and reciprocal communications; and since there is almost no way of raising taxes in a country with no accumulation of capital (*capitaux*), the central power cannot support a force considerable enough to maintain unity and obedience. In a great empire whose parts have almost no reciprocal connection, power remains in those areas where wealth is gathered and consumed; and if they are united, this can only be for their mutual security and by a federative pact.

The reign of the aristocracy lasts as long as agriculturists continue to be ignorant or neglectful of the skills of the artisan, and as long as landed property continues to be the only wealth.

As the natural development of societies is to grow ceaselessly in population and industry until they have attained the highest degree of civilization, the establishment of manufactures and of commerce should naturally succeed agriculture. However, two powerful forces can considerably hasten or retard the progress of this last epoch: the geographical situation, which calls men to commerce or isolates them, increases or prevents communication among them, opens or closes the sea to them; and political institutions, which make them esteem or despise commerce and direct their activity toward the arts of war, which diminish the population and inhibit wealth, or toward peaceful crafts which rapidly multiply men and goods.

In the long run political institutions adopt, so to speak, the genius of the locality. Sometimes, however, they may oppose it for a long period. Since the aristocracy before the era of commerce is, by the nature of things, in possession of power, it is the aristocracy that makes the laws, creates the prejudices, and controls the customs of the people. It has care, no doubt, to combine them in such a way as to perpetuate its power, and if it has as much cleverness as zeal in calculating the [appropriate] means, it may succeed in counterbalancing the influence of natural conditions through the energy of its institutions for a long time. Hence the inalienability of ecclesiastical estates, the right of primogeniture, entail, and so many other laws created by the feudal aristocracy at the time of its greatest power delayed its fall for several centuries. Thus Roman institutions had enough energy to preserve for six hundred years a contempt of arts and commerce in one of the regions of the world most perfectly situated for their cultivation.

Be that as it may, once the [mechanical] arts and commerce have succeeded in penetrating the people and creating a new means of wealth in support of the industrious class (*classe laborieuse*), a revolution in political laws is prepared. Just as the possession of land gave rise to the aristocracy, industrial property increases the power of the people: they acquire their liberty, they multiply, they begin to influence affairs.

[Thus, there emerges a] second kind of democracy. The first was independence, this one is strength; the first resulted from the absence of powers to oppress it, this one from a power which is its own; the first is that of barbaric, this one of civilized, peoples.

In small states, the strength [of the people] will be such that they may become at times master of the government. A new aristocracy, a sort of bourgeois and merchant aristocracy, may, it is true, arise through this new kind of wealth.

In large states, all elements are connected by reciprocal communication. A numerous class of citizens is formed which, with the great wealth of industry, has the greatest interest in maintaining internal order, and which by means of taxation provides public power with the necessary force to execute general laws and tie together all the parts. A considerable sum of taxes which is ceaselessly carried from the extremities to the center and from the center to the extremities, a regular army, a great capital, a multitude of public establishments; all become as many connections, giving a great nation that unity, that intimate cohesion [which renders its existence enduring].

Chapter IV

[*Application of These Ideas to Ancient States*]

These principles have some application to ancient history.

The small Greek states had kings during the heroic periods. They were nothing then but bands of adventurers, hunters, or wandering shepherds, and, always occupied with pillage and war, they needed chiefs. When they settled down to agriculture, they soon ceased to have kings, and aristocratic republics were formed in inland regions confined to agriculture, and democracies in the towns which engaged in commerce.

When the existence of Rome was consolidated and she ceased to fear her neighbors, and when the patricians had absorbed a great part of the lands of the poor, the aristocracy abolished royalty. Whatever credence may be given to the scandalous tyranny of the Tarquins and to the disinterested virtue of Brutus, if Rome had needed a king after the expulsion of Tarquin, she would soon have found a successor. If power had fallen into the hands of the aristocracy by a fortuitous circumstance and not by the nature of things, it would not have been maintained for several centuries. Democracy, which could never be entirely extinguished in Rome because the whole state consisted of a city, acquired immense power when capital flowed there through the progress of the arts and the despoiling of the world. Thus the influence of the people, the extent of the empire, and mercenary armies reestablished royalty there.

Carthage, having become a republic as soon as it was firmly established, also saw its government become more and more democratic as its commerce and wealth expanded.

Power seems to have other sources in the climates of Asia, and man appears constituted there to exist under monarchical government. However, the great despotic empires of the Orient, such as China and Hindostan today, seem to have achieved a degree of industry and wealth sufficient to sustain despotic authority: what proves it at least as well as the histories are the political maxims of antiquity, in which monarchical power is considered the effect of opulence, of luxury and softness. The people of the most fortunately situated countries of Asia seem to have achieved long ago a level of civilization which they cannot surpass: their physical disposition determines the level to which their wealth and arts can develop and is therefore an obstacle to both the power of wealth and to that energy of character by which a people succeed in tempering despotism with democracy.

Whatever is known to us of the great regions of the West is in keeping with what I have said of hunting and pastoral peoples and of those who have begun to practice agriculture.

Chapter V

[Application of the Same Ideas to Modern Europe]

But enough of these examples about which our notions are too uncertain and defective. The history of modern Europe is what is important to know well, and this very history gives the best evidence for the principles I have posited.

In the governments of Europe, the foundation of aristocracy is property in land; that of monarchy, public power; while the foundation of democracy is commercial wealth (*richesse mobilière*).

The revolutions of these three political elements have been those of governments.

When the feudal regime was at its highest level of power there was no property but in land. The equestrian and priestly aristocracy ruled over all; the people were reduced to slavery and the princes had no power.

The rebirth of the [mechanical] arts brought back industrial and commercial property, which is the fruit of labor, as landed property is originally the product of conquest or of occupation.

The democratic principle, then almost stifled, has since unceasingly gathered force and extended its own development. As the arts, industry, and commerce enrich the industrious class (*classe laborieuse*) of the people, impoverish the great landed proprietors, and bring the classes closer in wealth, the progress of education mutually assimilates their morals, and recalls after a long oblivion the primitive ideas of equality.

The great revolution which the influence of the progress of the arts has effected in European institutions may be divided into three branches.

1. The commons, acquiring wealth by labor, first bought their liberty and then a part of the land, while the aristocracy successively lost its domination and its wealth; thus the feudal regime crumbled under [the new] civil relationships.

2. The same cause, supported by the progress of industry which always accompanies it, freed the whole of Europe from the temporal power of the pope and took away half of his spiritual supremacy.

3. The same cause, that is to say the development (*progrès*) of commercial property, which is in Europe the element of democracy and the cement of the unity of states, successively modified all political governments. Accordingly as it was more or less favored by the geographical situation of [a given state], it established various governments. Where the people found

themselves very strong in a small state, republics were established; where, in an extensive area, they had only strength enough to sustain, by means of taxes, the monarchical power against the aristocracy, common enemy of prince and of people, they gradually established absolute monarchies. Where they were able to push their progress further, after having long served as the throne's accessory against the nobility, they caused an upheaval and, taking their place in the government, established limited monarchy. Only where their penetration was weak were the aristocratic and federative forms of feudal government able to maintain themselves and even acquire with time a more solid and regular form.

This is the sequence, common to all European governments, that prepared a democratic revolution in France and caused it to break out at the end of the eighteenth century.

These are the general ideas of which it remains to present the development and proof, by analyses and above all by examples and facts. The whole history of Europe is its demonstration. If some states seem to be exceptions to the general rule, it will be seen that the causes removing them from the general law are so evident, so [clear that they do not weaken the law].

Chapter VI

[*Development and Proof of the Preceding by Examples and Facts*]

The Romans conquered, civilized, disarmed the larger part of Europe. In bringing the [conquered] nations new skills, in debasing their courage and their morals, they rendered them incapable of defending themselves.

It appears that at this time the people inhabiting the northernmost regions of Europe had arrived at the degree of strength and population at which hunting and raising herds no longer sufficed for their subsistence. The sense of need therefore led them to seek satisfaction either in new crafts or in the possession of new lands. If these peoples had been kept within their geographical limits by the power of their neighbors they would have followed the natural development of societies. They would have been instructed by necessity in the cultivation of the soil, which would have provided for their increasing needs. But finding from the first attempts that the inhabitants of the South were incapable of defending their herds and their fertile lands, rather than new labors they preferred a mode of acquisition more in keeping with their penchants and their customs. They rushed on the Roman provinces in bands. The success of the first enterprises produced new ones. They moved from pillage to conquest: after trying profitable raids they attempted actual migrations, which better suited their needs. Whole peoples from the North moved to the South, occupying Roman provinces and establishing most of the states that divide the West today.

These new conquerors, far from bringing Europe new arts and riches, destroyed them; far from augmenting the population, [destroyed or dispersed it] by their ravages. Whatever was too refined, and as it were too fragile to be assimilated to their customs and levels of civilization, such as commerce, fine arts, and letters, disappeared as their incursions multiplied and their domination was consolidated. However, while the institutions of Europe declined, [those of the conquerors] made some progress through the appropriation and mixture of some of the usages of the vanquished. They brought with them the morals and independence of a savage and warrior people; they received from the vanquished both religion and the cultivation of the soil. It was the combined domination of these three elements that constituted feudal government.

In the natural development (*progrès*) of societies, although the cultivation of the soil precedes manufacturing industry and commerce, these phases follow one upon the other rather closely. Thus, by the time an extensive region is entirely cultivated, the arts have already made enough progress so that the resulting political effect already gives the people some power, and palpably balances and moderates the results of an exclusively agricultural [situation].

A people naturally arrived at this stage might at the same time have acquired more perfected institutions which would diminish its abuses. They would form only small states, in which the common will could have some energy and could temper the influence of the rich. Finally, following the natural progression, they would soon attain civilized customs.

The circumstances of conquest change these effects, and the moderate aristocracy which naturally emerges in the third period of human societies becomes instead a tyranny. . . .

Here are the main points of these circumstances:

1. When, by the successive effects of conquest, Europe arrived at the condition of peoples who no longer practiced any art but agriculture, this was not through the common progress of the whole nation but the effect of the mixture of two races of men, one of which came from a highly advanced state of civilization and the other from a much more barbarous condition. [This happened] in such a way that the vanquished brought all the weakness . . . of a degenerate people to this mixture, and the conquerors all the barbarism of a [young] people.

2. Conquest always produces great inequality in the division of wealth: not only does conquest despoil the vanquished; among the victors it hardly enriches anyone but the chiefs. The soldier scarcely finds enough in his portion to sustain his arrogant indolence for a short time.

3. The way in which [the conquest] was made aggravated these effects. The conquest had not been the result of a single invasion, like those rapid revolutions which change almost nothing in the state of things, and subjecting the vanquished to the domination of the victor, almost always subject the victor to the morals and usages of the vanquished. A long series of successive incursions, lengthy dissensions among various colonies of conquerors, desolated Europe for two centuries. Its wealth was

destroyed, its population disappeared; and what was then, as always, the effect of war among peoples, a considerable part of the remaining population was reduced to slavery.

4. When men arrive naturally at the third stage of society, that of cultivation of the land, they abandon a large part of the area they have possessed as wanderers. Coming together in groups, cultivating only a small part of the terrain, they form small states whose center is a rising town. [At this stage of society] the common will has some power over the influence of the rich. But when the barbarians—hunters or shepherds in their homelands—inundated Europe, they traversed it with a rapidity typical of their customs. Nations of a few hundred thousand men covered immense regions and founded vast states, during a period of social organization in which some degree of order and liberty could prevail only in very small groups.

As long as some debris of wealth remained—the arts and civilization of the vanquished—aristocracy was tempered and the people still retained some strength.

As long as the conquering nations disputed the great regions of Europe, each of them, whether for conquest or defense, found it necessary to maintain unity and to give some authority to its chief. Thus monarchical power, subject to frequent revolutions, nevertheless preserved the necessary energy to assure common defense or acquisitions, and in the interval which separated the invasion of the empire and the perfect establishment of feudal government, aristocracy was still quite limited. But gradually two results occurred: commerce and the arts, steadily retreating before the ravages of war and the barbarian morals of the conquerors, finally disappeared; and commercial wealth, the kind of property which is the fruit of labor, which is the share of the active and industrious part of the people and makes for its strength and its liberty—which finally, as I shall soon prove, is the principal cement of the unity of states—was completely annihilated. With it disappeared the liberty of the people and the internal order of states.

The great empires of Europe were established, the nations

settled on their territory existed within themselves and ceased [their constant warfare].

From this it resulted that monarchical power, being less necessary, had less energy, and its bonds, which were based on the necessity of common defense, relaxed. Then Europe found itself divided into large monarchies, where the prince had almost no power and the people were without industry. [There appeared] two classes of men, one with the power of arms, which is everything in a country where the public power has no energy; the other with the force of superstition, so [prominent] among a people of extreme ignorance. Together they possessed the land, which then formed the only wealth and by the nature of things carried with it all power. They soon succeeded in subjugating the people, in freeing themselves from the control of the prince, and—by their progress, by the hierarchy that developed among them, by the laws they created to regularize this strange regime— founded what we call feudal government.

I have said that in a country where the only property is in land and where industrial work is unknown, large properties gradually tend to absorb small ones. But [this process], which is effected only by legal means in a country where public authority has some force and customs tend toward refinement, would be accomplished in quicker and more violent ways in large monarchies where the prince is without power and the customs of part of the nation are still almost as barbaric as at its origin.

Such was the nature of the feudal regime. It achieved the highest degree of force and intensity at the moment when the barbarians had destroyed all traces of the arts and commerce and when the advances [of society] had not yet begun to reproduce them.

These advances had to be slow, for the very conditions which had plunged all of Europe into slavery, ignorance, and feudal anarchy tended to perpetuate [these evils]. But the gradual influence of nature always prevails in the long run over that of accidental causes. Men, changed by great events, return little by little to what the soil, the climate, and all general causes demand that they be. Nature destined the Europeans to surpass all inhabitants of the globe in their active industry, or at least all those of the ancient world. Her design was that the temperate zone, which in Asia includes only interior lands and in Africa does not exist, would in Europe be interspersed with seas, gulfs, lakes, and a multitude of navigable rivers. [Thus, here] where the temperature of the climate gives man more strength and activity, the nature of the soil assures more fertility to the land, more means of commercial communication; and . . . the two great factors that modify human nature, the influence of the sky and the land, combine to give to the [inhabiting] peoples the whole range of faculties of which they are capable.

Industry and the [practical] arts therefore had to be reborn here; and if they were held back by the feudal regime, the debris of the arts and sciences of the Greeks and Romans which remained in the East, transported by various means to the West, contributed to accelerate their growth.

Unhappy circumstance which, with so many others, has dictated that in our sciences and our arts, as in our languages, morals, and institutions, nothing is indigenous, nothing is primitive, but [rather] the fruit of a thousand different sources, altered and corrupted by one another! We exhausted in vain imitations the age in which our genius had all its strength. When we began [to see] that nature was the true model, we no longer had the youth that can perceive and paint her. Genius and taste, which among the Greeks existed together, have been successive among us. A most remarkable thing, that the only one of the fine arts of which the ancients left no model is the first and perhaps the only one in which the moderns have excelled: that is, painting.

The abstract sciences were long corrupted by the same cause but the evil was less, because in the natural advance of societies their reign [that of the sciences] comes later than that of works of imagination and sentiment. We mis-reasoned in an age when nations do not yet know how to reason at all. We have since corrected our errors; but we wasted in false knowledge and feeble imitations the period destined for perceiving and depicting nature: [that] precious age which, like the passions of youth, once past never returns.

But along with these works which are the most brilliant and magnificent part of human genius come some of a more ordinary usefulness, whose influence on morals and governments is more powerful because more general. These are the practical arts, the trades, commerce in all its parts, and those of the sciences which are applied directly to the simplification and perfection of these arts. Nothing having contravened the development (*progrès*) of the peoples of Europe along these lines of industry and knowledge, to which nature seems particularly to have destined them, they had hardly emerged from feudal anarchy when their progress became rapid and universal. This must be considered a principal factor which, over a period of four to five centuries, has modified all governments and changed the face of Europe.

I have said that landed property, when its influence is not limited and modified by industrial wealth, is the principle of aristocracy, because its primary origin dates from conquest or from an occupation which favors only a small number; because its natural development is the invasion of small properties by large ones; because its nature is to give dominion and military power to those who possess it.

Industrial wealth, on the contrary, is the portion of the industrious (*laborieuse*) element of the people. Its origin is work. Through it the rich become dependent on the industry of the poor. Through it the industrious poor man gradually draws to himself parcels of the property of the rich and ends by acquiring some portion of their lands. Through it he acquires, in favorable circumstances, the education and pride that follow in its wake. Through [this wealth] the people unite in those great manufacturing workshops which are called towns, and succeed by their unity in opposing an effective resistance to the oppression of the great proprietors. Industrial and commercial property is therefore the principle of democracy, as landed property is the principle of aristocracy.

I have said that in a large state where there exists no industry but the cultivation of the land, and consequently no property other than landed property, the social bond and, so to speak, the cohesion among the different parts can only be very weak.

INTRODUCTION TO THE FRENCH REVOLUTION 93

Industry and commercial property produce the opposite effect. Through them the objects of exchange multiply, great wealth is easily transferred, distances diminish, a continuous circulation is established among all the parts of an empire, [and] with the accumulation of capital (*capitaux*) the state is able to acquire, through taxation, the means to support a civil government and an army, which belongs not to each section that provides it but to the whole society. A large class of citizens is formed, devoted to commerce and manufacture, which, having a great need of peace and protection, through the grant of taxes furnishes the government with the means of acquiring adequate strength.

In large states, therefore, just as landed property is the basis of aristocracy and federalism, commercial property is the principle of democracy and of unity.

It is interesting to observe how this political factor has shaped all European governments for five hundred years, [to see its] general effects over such a large part of the earth, its diverse consequences resulting from particular conditions and from the geographic situation of each state which has given it more or less energy and [has] more or less hastened or retarded the epoch of its power. Sometimes it works in a slow and imperceptible manner; sometimes, when the accumulated force [of the principle of commercial property] becomes superior to the obstacles that have contained it, it explodes suddenly and violently, changing the face of empires and the whole of Europe.

While the people grew rich through labor and the [mechanical] arts, multiplied in the towns, and prepared to acquire landed property and divide it into small portions, the nobles, becoming daily enslaved to new enjoyments, consumed in the demands of a novel luxury the revenues which, when consecrated to hospitality and war, had been the basis of their power. Gradually they became too weak to control their vassals, who, with greater population and ease of life, acquired a spirit of liberty. Too poor to sustain their new magnificence, they gradually sold to their subjects the rights which in the nature of things it was no longer possible to refuse them. Freedom and division of lands followed the progress of personal liberty. The man who under slavery has cultivated the earth for his master, gaining part of his liberty through his savings, will no longer labor without self-interest, and becomes a kind of share-cropper. Acquiring his full liberty through his accumulated profits, he also acquires landed property through the payment of a quit rent.

These civil consequences, this reversal in the means of acquisition, this change in the reciprocal relationships of the people and nobles, has taken place in all countries subject to the feudal regime. Wherever political events and geographical situation encouraged the development (*progrès*) of industry, commerce, and the arts, this revolution which changed the condition of men was more rapid and complete.

The same cause had other effects in the political system and government of states. In small territories where an advantageous situation lent it great force, [commercial property] gave all power to the people and created republics. In large states where the countryside necessarily had a greater influence than the towns, where the center of power could exist only in the chief of the army, the political force resulting naturally from the enfranchisement and wealth of the people was concentrated in the monarch. With the mandate of protecting the civil rights of his subjects against anarchy and aristocracy, he received from them the largest share in the exercise of political power. Through the taxes he received from the people, he won back from the hands of the nobles their military power, the exercise of justice, and a more or less extended portion of the legislative power. Some notable differences appeared among the various monarchies, but as these are all completely relative to the degree of energy exerted by the general principle, far from casting doubt on its influence, they are its best demonstration. The general account I shall soon sketch will carry [this demonstration to the strongest proofs]; but I shall first describe a third revolution brought about in the situation of Europe by the same cause.

Chapter VII

[*Consequences to Religion of the Progress of Civilization*]

There are three connected elements which follow the progress of human civilization simultaneously. These are population, wealth, and the independence of public opinion.

With the [mechanical] arts, which enrich us and increase the numbers of men by increasing the means of subsistence, are born those higher forms of knowledge which expose credulity to the light of reason. Boldness of thought, like all types of courage, is a product of the feeling of power; public opinion arises naturally in a wealthy and numerous people—a large population enjoying comfort and leisure. It is like a spirituous substance which is born and developed by fermentation in a large aggregate of men.

The progress of industry and commercial wealth which freed the people and reduced the nobles, [and] constituted states under more or less regular forms, had finally, therefore, to break the bonds of superstition and sap the base of power which had been acquired by the ministers of the Catholic religion.

The revolution that weakened the clergy was related, like the one that weakened the domination of the nobles, to general circumstances; [it] had a more uniform development than the revolution that changed the forms of government. Both were presaged in Europe by remarkable crises which may be considered the greatest events of modern history. I refer to the Crusades and to Luther's reform.

Neither the humiliations suffered by the pilgrims at the hands of the Turks, nor the preaching of Peter the Hermit, nor the scandal of indulgences and the resentment of the monk Luther were the true causes of these great explosions.

When [the time is ripe for change] there will always be some incident to precipitate it.

From a certain point of view such concepts as population, wealth, morals, enlightenment, may be considered as the elements and the substance that form the body social, while laws and government may be seen as the tissue that contains and envelops them. In every state of society there must be a proportion of force and area between the two. If the tissue expands as the volume of the substance is augmented, the development of the body social takes place without violent upheaval; but if, instead of an elastic strength, it offers a brittle rigidity, the moment will come when all proportions cease and, if the humor is not dissipated, it will rupture its envelope and extravasate.

Accidental circumstances surrounding the crisis do not cause, but may influence it.

We have seen that the northern barbarians, when their institutions ceased to fit their population and needs, finding the borders of the South undefended, inundated it. Had they been confined to their territory, their force would have been turned inward and thus changed their social regime. I shall recount later how a great European empire verged on a revolution in its government, when the force which should have accomplished it found issue in the discovery of the New World (perhaps the most beautiful site in the universe, this land which was the fatherland of liberty) and instead rushed there. How many internal revolutions have been prevented or retarded by these long and bloody wars, which, consuming both wealth and population, open a great career to the restlessness of genius and seem to augment the power of government in the same proportion as they diminish that of peoples!

When the narrow and rigid bonds of the feudal regime could no longer contain the mass of population, industry, and activity which the early advances of civilization had produced in Europe, the Crusades occurred: a fortunate and salutary crisis which hastened but also softened the revolution that was to achieve the liberation of the commons. The natural restlessness (*inqui-*

étude naturelle) of peoples subject to a government which no longer suited them caused them to be drawn toward the east by accidental factors, where a part of the population remained. Thus one of the elements that ordinarily change the shape [of governments] diminished and slackened. On the other hand, the lords, in order to provide for the expenses of these distant expeditions, met the desires of their vassals and accorded them, in return for gold, an abandonment of those harsh exactions which they could no longer maintain. In this way a part of the ferment of revolution was dissipated, and the rest worked its effect without violence by means of peaceful arrangements.

The clergy had acquired immense wealth and had founded an absurd and excessive power on the general ignorance, on the weakness of the people and the [degradation] in which royal authority had been kept by the feudal regime. An odious tyranny oppressed kings, nobles, and people, appropriated their riches, exercised or assigned all political and civil authority. That authority, contrary to the interest of all, could exist only as long as the means which had established it continued to have force. From the time when enlightenment began to spread, when the liberated people came to know comfort and sensed their strength, when the kings, emerging from tutelage, could exercise an independent power, this immense edifice no longer had any foundation, and the slightest blow was enough to overturn it. Thus the first words of Luther were like a spark that fell on [a mass of] combustible materials. From the beginning of the Roman Church a multitude of sectaries had attacked it: several [among] them seem not to have been inferior to the leader of the Reformation in either character or talent, and yet, despite their efforts, the Roman Church did not cease to expand. But when the time of its decadence, marked by the nature of things, had arrived [although the Church was] at the summit of its apparent grandeur, a single man became formidable to it. Each of his apostles or imitators who succeeded him had the power to convert peoples and make revolutions. Half of Europe followed the innovators and escaped from the Roman Church; and if she kept the rest, it was through the successive abandonment of her most precious rights—the steady sacrifice of the reality of power to preserve its appearance.

It is enough to have shown these two great crises which marked the weakening of the power of the nobles and the authority of the priesthood. I shall not pursue the vicissitudes endured by each of these powers in the various states. They are connected with the revolutions of their governments, are part of them, and will find their place in the sketch I shall make of the development of each. One should not expect to find this immense picture in a few pages; I can only indicate the outlines and some of its characteristic features, useful in casting new light on the general principles I have stated.

Chapter VIII

[Democratic Influences: The Italian and Flemish Republics]

Industry and commerce are the principle of commercial wealth and of the people's strength. The democratic influence, therefore, necessarily became evident in the various states more or less rapidly and with more or less force according as their geographic situation and other less powerful factors summoned these states sooner or later to the cultivation of the arts and to navigation.

Italy was situated on the world's most navigable sea. She had been the seat of the empire; civilization, the arts and wealth which had there been carried to the highest level had to leave some traces. Placed near the eastern empire, where the remains of human industry had taken refuge, everything passing to the West had to stop there necessarily. Finally, amid the general barbarism some commercial [relations] had survived between East and West, and Italy was their center and natural entrepôt.

She was therefore [the most advanced] of all the regions of Europe.

Read her history and you will see in her political institutions all the results necessarily produced by the conditions of her civilization.

The feudal regime never had great strength there and did hardly more, so to speak, than to pass over. The priesthood, which because of the proximity of the Holy See should have exercised great influence on opinion, usurped less property and power there than in any other part of Europe; among her numerous prelates only the bishop of Rome became a temporal prince. The freedom, influence, and power of the towns existed earlier and to a greater extent than in any other region. All of Europe was still in servitude when Italy already had several democratic republics, completely independent, some of which soon ranked among the most powerful states.

After the trade between East and West of which Italy was the center, the most natural and important was the exchange of the products of the North and South. Italy, which had the entrepôt of the East and all the surviving manufactures, was the southern terminus at which this commerce necessarily concentrated. But another had to be established in the North, and thus [there appeared] the Hanseatic towns, their commerce, their wealth, and their freedom.

They practiced commerce, industry, and the arts in the midst of centuries of ignorance and barbarism; and as a result of this principle they possessed liberty.

The towns of the Low Countries were favored by the elements that founded the Hanseatic towns, and even more by the proximity of England, rich in raw materials which she did not yet know how to manufacture. Thus they were the first, after those I have cited, where industry and wealth accumulated and where the spirit of freedom and the efforts of democracy made themselves felt. A part of this country liberated itself and has founded the most powerful republic in Europe.

The part of the Low Countries which has remained under the power of kings, nobles, and the clergy is a country more agricultural than commercial, because of the fertility and depth of its soils. Its disadvantage lies in the fact that of all the regions of Europe it is the most accessible to invading armies. Finally, its history by no means contradicts the principles I have enunciated. If democracy has lost its strength there, this has been in proportion to the decline of commerce and the arts. It has been observed in recent times that the maritime province whose towns were formerly so flourishing is where democratic principles had the most access, while in the interior provinces the privileged have preserved the greatest ascendancy.

Chapter IX

General Ideas on the Republics [of Europe]

I must anticipate some objections, which one might base on the very example of these republics, against the principle I have posed that commerce, industry, in a word commercial property, is in Europe the principle of democracy and the bond of unity of states.

In effect all or almost all of these republics are today more or less aristocratic. The Hanseatic towns, independently of their connection with the empire, have long maintained a political league among themselves; and the United Provinces, which have the world's greatest accumulation of commercial property, are still ruled by a federative government. The example of landlocked Switzerland, existing for several centuries under a republican and even, in part, democratic form of government, will be held up against [my principle]; [also] that of Geneva [and] the imperial cities situated in the interior of Germany. I am the less disposed to evade these objections, since what is necessary to clarify them will illumine in advance what I shall have to say about monarchies.

The aristocracy which today rules most of the republics of

Europe has nothing in common with the equestrian and feudal nobility.

Most of these republics began in a truly democratic spirit. However, commerce, which at first had been the basis of the people's strength and emancipation, soon led some families to the acquisition of excessive wealth; they gradually usurped public authority and succeeded through various means in rendering the magistracies hereditary. Thus appeared that bourgeois aristocracy which ordinarily becomes the dominating element in commercial republics. But, although affecting the title of noble and others even more pompous, it is nevertheless essentially as different in its nature as in its origins from the equestrian aristocracy which arises from the exercise of arms and the possession of land.

Pure democracy is so violent a condition in a country where extreme poverty and narrow territorial limits do not preserve the simplicity of morals and equality of fortunes appropriate to it, that as soon as a state begins to be agitated by factions arising from wealth and the corruption of morals it necessarily succumbs to monarchy or aristocracy.

In Italy the republic of Florence, which escaped aristocracy, the natural result of its great commerce, fell under the domination of the Medicis.

But it is no less true that all these republics were founded by democracy. In general, the two great springs of power are military force and money; but in commercial republics only the latter, so to speak, exists. The rich capitalists, having nothing above them, become an aristocracy in relation to the people, while in monarchies they remain [part of the] democracy, in opposition to the equestrian nobility and military power.

The federation under which several republics of Europe exist also belongs by nature to republican government, and does not negate the principle I have posed, that commercial wealth is the bond of the unity of states.

Here is how this is explained.

In general, nothing is less disposed to a federation than a commercial republic. Since all power there concentrates in the towns, and as the first characteristic distinguishing merchants is an extreme jealousy, it is certain that the most powerful will want to dominate and destroy the others. If they cannot be subjugated, they separate—unless a very powerful external cause arises to oppose these natural tendencies.

Whatever the government of a country, and from whatever source those who rule hold power, there are two means—or, if one may so express it, two principal instruments—through which they exercise it: these are men and wealth, military power and money.

These two means of governing being the principal springs of power, the way in which they exist and are distributed in each country must powerfully influence the form of its constitution. For example, it is clear that no government can spread beyond the extent of territory which can be dominated by the instrument of power proper to it.

I have said—leaving aside the Swiss, who form an exception to the system of our modern institutions—that all our European republics were founded on the [mechanical] arts and commerce. Now, the first law of a commercial republic is that it must have no army, or at least that the military power must be extremely subordinate. It is therefore evident, as I shall prove in a moment, that a commercial republic can contain only that extent of territory which it is possible to hold together by the power of wealth alone. But I must first prove the preceding proposition.

In all countries where there is a considerable armed force its influence necessarily dominates. Power goes to those who possess it. Therefore it is necessary either that the constitution give power to those who control the army or that the army change the constitution.

Thus, in military republics like Rome and Lacedaemon, the people themselves make up the army.

Thus, in feudal government in its various periods, the exercise of military power is at the discretion of the proprietors of fiefs; thus in monarchy the king is essentially head of the army.

But in commercial republics the people, whether laboring, manufacturing, or mercantile, are not soldierly, and their magistrates are not captains. Existence, wealth, and power are based on peaceful arts. Armed force is, in a sense, alien to government and does not enter into its composition. If it exists alongside the government it must attack and destroy it.

For this reason it is difficult for a country much exposed to invasions to exist in the form of a commercial republic, since the means necessary to its security tend to change its constitution. One may observe that Holland, although protected by water and the infertility of her soil, was always led by wars to reestablish the stadtholderate and give it more power. Where an army is necessary, it must have a constitutional leader, or there will always be the fear that its temporary chief may become a tyrant.

At certain times commercial republics attain excessive wealth, and the effect is usually ambition for conquest. This is an illusion which must lead to their ruin. One must study the policies of Carthage and of Venice toward their armies and their generals, and the striking opposition that developed between their desire to conquer, on the one hand, and their mistrust and suspicion of armed force on the other. Both waging war with foreign mercenaries, one commanded them by its citizens, while the other was careful to give command only to adventurers of no consideration; but this apart, their concern to contain, oversee, and degrade their generals was the same. Thus, besides the danger of losing domestic liberty through the audacious stroke of one of their chiefs, they ran the increased danger of seeing their independence compromised by their neighbors. They aroused all the hatred and jealousy resulting from their unchecked desires for aggrandizement, but never dared give their military forces the energy and development of which they were capable. In this way Carthage perished; having excited the hatred of Rome, she had the opportunity to annihilate her rival, but her jealousy of Hannibal prevented her profiting from it. Having sacrificed to her internal policy the means of pursuing external successes as far as possible, she herself soon succumbed to an enemy victorious in its turn, [an enemy] which, because of the spirit of its constitution, did not have to observe the same precautions.

The history of Venice is almost the same: having called forth a league through its ambition, its defective military regime left it almost without defense in the moment of danger. Venice escaped the final misfortune, it is true, but she owed this to her enemies rather than to her own resources. Between Carthage's fate and hers there was only this difference, that Carthage had to fight a single rival which never had any interest or policy but to destroy her; while Venice, fortunately, had to deal with a league, and at the moment of her ruin her enemies, having different views and varying interests, saved her by their divisions.

But it is nonetheless true that, long before the time when her real power was undermined by the diversion of her commerce, she had lost her mainland conquests, which were acquired and preserved by military force. She possessed no more than the limited area which could be dominated by a powerful city, and her distant possessions, which she could control and defend with her fleet.

In fact, by an opulent city's ascendancy over the lands and small towns in its vicinity, which it dominates and enriches, and by its maritime power, a commercial republic can replace that instrument so dangerous to it: a strong army. A powerful fleet is the natural result of an extensive commerce, of great wealth and developed industry; it conforms perfectly to these elements [of economic strength]; it is most suitable to the acquisition and protection of establishments useful for commerce. A fleet does not menace civil liberty, and most of the men it employs are of a condition subordinate to the merchant citizen; it fulfills his needs.

The unity of the state demands a central power which strongly attracts all factions and subordinates them to its influence. Since in monarchies the center is a king, and since the most essential characteristic of royalty is command of the army, monarchical unity can extend over the whole area of a territory which a large army can control. But in republics the center of the state's unity can only be a town, and in those especially which are based on commerce the existence of a strong army is incompatible with their constitution. Political unity therefore cannot extend beyond that area which a large town could dominate without the use of an army, and this is the absolute limit of unity in commercial republics.

If a larger state finds itself led by events to the republican form, and if the dangers to which it is exposed from its neighbors preclude its division into as many independent states as there are large towns, it will federate: such is the government of Holland.

If Holland[1] had no dangerous neighbors, including as it does a territory too large for one town to dominate, and several towns important enough for each to form the center of a state, it is probable that she would divide into several republics, completely distinct and rivals. Federative government is maintained there, despite the natural effect of commerce, by external dangers. Moreover, if the stadtholder could succeed in drawing to himself the power of gold as he has that of armed force, this federation would soon give way to a monarchical unity.

We conclude from these observations that aristocracy and federation, which are seen in some of the European commercial republics, do not controvert the general principles I have posited above: first, because their aristocracy has nothing in common with feudal aristocracy, being only in a sense a degenerate democracy; second, because their federation does not come from their own disposition but from the small territory allowed by republican government, as compared to what their security imperiously demands. Thus it may be said that in these states external influence does violence to the spirit of internal government.

1. Properly, the (seven) United Provinces (of which Holland was the most important).

Chapter X

[General Ideas on Monarchies]

We pass to monarchies.

In every government with some monarchical element there is a center of power, extremely forceful and influential, which tends to draw all authority to itself and thus promote the unity of the state.

The progress of commercial wealth first gives it the means to increase this power by weakening the aristocracy. Thus the feudal monarchies pass from aristocratic federation to monarchical unity.

If the dispositions of the state are such that the people acquire greater power than the military force controlled by the prince, democracy takes its place in the government and the monarchy will combine with a national representation.

If, on the contrary, the nature of things limits popular development (*progrès*) and gives armed force great energy, the latter acquiring a decided superiority in the hands of the prince, monarchical unity will degenerate into a military despotism.

There is not a page of modern history which fails to testify to these truths. Let us further clarify these ideas before giving examples.

When no arts, nor commerce, nor commercial wealth existed, there were no circulation and no taxes. States were unable to undertake anything beyond their borders and had almost nothing to fear from their neighbors: they existed and acted within themselves. Such wealth as there was, military power, and consequently public power, remained in the hands of the large landed proprietors. The people were enslaved and the prince was without power.

The people, acquiring some wealth with the progress of industry, conceded a part of it to the prince in order to obtain his protection against the tyranny of the nobles. The latter saw their wealth diminish by the same development. The prince, strong through the support of the people, and above all through the weakening of the nobility, saw his authority emerge from a long tutelage.

With the revenue of taxes he established and paid judges and the whole machine of government. But he did something more important: he changed the nature of armies, and it was this instrument above all which made the revolution in governments.

Since a large army, where it exists, is the principal basis of power, the manner of its organization must influence the distribution of authority.

There are two kinds of armed force, essentially distinct:

The first is composed of regular troops, a body of men drawn indifferently from all regions of a state, employed in continuous service, paid and commanded by the power that dominates in the center of the empire. Since such an army is but a body of inhabitants from all the provinces, since it belongs to the whole nation and obeys a single authority, always ready to subject each part to the will that governs the whole, it will be easily understood that this is a powerful bond of unity.

Such an army, rallying to the central will, which is for it always the will of its leader, is essentially monarchical.

The second kind of armed force is what is called in European governments a militia. I understand by this term any armed force in which each corps is raised in one canton of the state, commanded by officers of the same canton, which is not employed in the general service of the state save in moments of need, and not paid by the public treasury except in its short intervals of service.

As much as the first kind of army tends toward unity, the latter inclines toward federation. It is easily seen that [the militia] cannot form a well-amalgamated whole, that each corps belongs less to the state than to its canton, that the troops depend less on their common chief, and on the general with whom their relations are as rare as they are distant, than on the officers living among them and strengthening each day the bonds of authority or confidence.

The armed force of feudal times was completely of the kind last described: never subsidized by the state, serving only in the moment of need, commanded by nobles, composed of men some of whom were their vassals and others their slaves [the feudal host] depended only on them, obeyed only them. [The feudal seigneurs] thus retained authority in each fief, [and were] united among themselves and with their common chief by that federative bond of which fidelity and homage were the expression.

When the kings obtained subsidies from the commons, enriched by the rebirth of the arts, they began to form and hire regular troops. These new forces, more trained, always active, subjected to a more exacting discipline, commanded by a single will, increased in number as the taxation that supported them grew with the public wealth. At first they balanced, then surpassed, then caused the total disappearance of the feudal militia. In this development authority passed from the hands of the nobles commanding it to the king, the general of these new forces.

Here are found nuances of difference between the monarchies whose consequences, at first small but steadily increasing, finally lead some to military despotism and others to a well-organized liberty.

The basis of aristocracy is land; the basis of monarchy, public force; the basis of democracy is commercial wealth.

There are empires in which the influence of the land so dominates that the monarchical principle, [barely] sustained by the weak efforts of the people, never gets the upper hand. Their fate is to remain in a kind of feudal federation, superficially mollified by the morals of our century. Their subsequent fate will be perhaps conquest at the time when surrounding governments achieve an energy which overbalances their extreme weakness.

There are some [empires] where forces are so distributed that the people have been able to acquire enough to give royalty the means to crush the aristocracy [but] never enough to struggle against the monarch themselves. Democratic and aristocratic forces being equally balanced, the royal power, raising itself above both, paralyzes one by means of the other and succeeds in subjugating them. First it depresses the nobles with the people's money; then it defeats the people with the spirit of the nobles, who degenerate into a kind of military servitude. For the nobility is as ready to ally with the prince against the people when it fears their dominance as it is to subjugate the royal power through its own efforts. The destiny of these states is to move by a slow progression from feudal anarchy to the most absolute military regime.

Finally there are empires protected by their situation from the plague of war. War is always favorable to kings, depositaries of the public power, and to the nobles, whose landed property cannot be destroyed; but it is destructive to the people, whose labor demands tranquillity and leads to navigation and commerce. [In such activities] by the nature of things, commercial wealth and consequently the power of the people must acquire an immense scope. [In these empires] the people, granting the prince money to pay his army and govern the state, will one day acquire sufficient force to deny it to him. [The people] will state conditions, will want to examine its [the money's] use, and will demand that the authority it supports be organized for their own advantage. They will want to conduct their own affairs in those departments where they have the ability to do so, and to exercise surveillance over those they cannot manage. Thus the free and limited monarchy is formed, the happiest and most advantageous of governments that has ever ruled the earth.

Royal power will be based on needs recognized by all and on the influence of all parts of the government of which it will be the trustee.

Popular power . . .

The aristocracy, if it continues to exist, will be held to those limits which will prevent its harmful effects while rendering it useful. Deprived of the hope of increasing its power, which always makes it factious, it will exist on the defensive and will become the ballast of government. Placed between two stronger and more active powers which influence it, one by public opinion and the other by the distribution of honors, it will bind them together and soften their more violent conflicts through its conservative restraint.

Unity will be powerfully supported by the interest of the two dominant powers, the king's and the people's. The size of the territory will require that the people be part of the government, through representative institutions . . .

I cannot tear myself from this picture. O peoples whom nature has allowed to arrive at this form of government, whatever the sacrifices it has cost you, you have not bought it too dear!

Although each of the European monarchies is drawn by its situation toward one of these three results, it is nevertheless true that great political events may sometimes make them deviate for a while from the course assigned them by general causes. In most states there comes a moment when—the aristocracy [being] weakened but not destroyed, and the prince and the people strengthened—the influence of the three powers achieves a kind of equilibrium, although without the government being accordingly organized. Accidental causes may then decide which [force will assume control over the others]. Profiting by the triumph gained through circumstances to strengthen itself and weaken the others, it [that force] will give the development of government a direction different from that destined for it by the nature of things.

Such is the influence of despotism that if, aided by accidental conditions, it succeeds in predominating for some time, its compressive force will arrest the progress of population and wealth or even make them retrogress, thus prolonging its [own] dominance despite the influence of locale and climate.

Similarly, if the people, aided by events contrary to the natural course, prevail, turning the spirit of government toward labor and acquisition—dilating, so to speak, the fibers of the body politic—a new nourishment of men and of wealth will be introduced, making it possible to support a form of government established by fortuitous causes against the nature of things.

Similarly with the aristocracy; we have seen how, favored by the barbarian invasions, it instituted usages and laws which made for its dominance over several centuries.

But the error committed by historians in the interpretation of modern history is that they have attributed almost everything to these accidental causes. However, while it is true to say that they are all-powerful for a moment, or, if you like, in determining the time of revolutions, they change almost nothing in the long run or in important results.

I will be asked where, in this picture of monarchies, I place Montesquieu's. It belongs precisely at the point which I have just described, where the government, emerging from feudalism, moves toward another, as yet undeveloped form in which the aristocracy has ceased to be tyrannical, in which the prince is not yet a despot nor the people free. An epoch in which royal power dominates, restricted by the memory of the nobles' power and by public opinion, which is the prelude to the power of the people.

Respect and honors, which emerge after power [is won], also survive its demise for some time. A knightly nobility's code will reign for some time after its real basis of power has disappeared. Its honors, its maxims, and its example are then the most powerful of the moral principles giving impulsion to government; and this was also Montesquieu's doctrine.

But M. de Montesquieu seems to have made a [definite form of] government of what is only a precarious condition, a transition between two more determinate forms of government. He described the situation in which he saw several European states at the time he wrote, without considering that this condition could not last because it rested on a current of opinion whose basis no longer existed, and that before long the monarchy would need other limits and other bases. Montesquieu's monarchy tends toward military despotism or toward limited monarchy (*monarchie organisée*).

This part of his book, the least attractive, won him the most partisans because it flattered the ideas and interests of a multitude of personages. How many people have retained from the *Spirit of the Laws* only this adage: "No monarchy without nobility"?

But if this maxim were rigorously true how could it be, following M. de Montesquieu himself, that despotic government, in which the power of the prince comes to its height, cannot allow the existence of a nobility?[2]

Chapter XI

[*Application of the Preceding to the Inland States of Europe and to the Maritime States*]

Let us follow the application of these ideas to the different European monarchies.

[1. *Inland States*]

Inland states without access to the sea are the ones where the aristocracy's domination necessarily persisted and where the people were unable to acquire enough force even to fortify royal power against their tyrants.

Observe the political condition of Germany, Poland, or Hungary until the middle of the last century—the three large inland regions of Europe.

After the barbarian conquest and under the feudal regime, the government of these countries was very similar to those of other European countries.

---

2. Probably a somewhat sophistical misconstrual of Montesquieu's concept of despotism, which he sharply distinguished from monarchy through its lack of "fundamental laws."

INTRODUCTION TO THE FRENCH REVOLUTION 113

But while those with access to the sea tended, through the progress of commerce and industry, toward a form of government more favorable to the people and royalty, the aristocracy of the land-locked states preserved and steadily extended its power and independence. The power of electing kings remained with them. They [those states] continued to be forms of aristocratic federation under the direction of an elective chief.

I cannot conceive how some very clever historians have been able to attribute aristocratic federation, which in Germany was the product of centuries, to the quarrels of emperors and popes; as if so [trivial] a cause could have had any influence! As if the government of Poland, where the kings have never had any entanglement with the heads of the Church, were not of the same nature as that of the [Holy Roman] empire, with this difference, that being more completely inland, more deprived of commerce by its position, its free cities were even weaker and its constitution more perfectly aristocratic.

Here I cannot deny myself an observation on the German empire which is not foreign to my subject. Among the determining conditions that give so much renown and endurance to the European political system, none is perhaps more influential than the geographical situation, having in the center a large region, fertile and rich, inhabited by a valiant nation, but whose form of government dictates a defensive system. I find that Germany is the fixed center of Europe and the surrounding empires the moving parts. Her ponderous and conservative constitution prevents her from invading the surrounding areas, and her impenetrable strength prevents the states which she separates from striking at each other.

Royal power has made some progress in Hungary, but it is evident that this results from a cause which in all other countries would have established the most absolute despotism—from the policy of the house of Austria, which, possessed of a number of kingdoms for several centuries, has been able to subjugate some through the others. The very great strength preserved by the nobility in that country [Hungary], and the elective nature of the crown, maintained until the middle of the last century, prove with what force the nature of the locale conflicts with a power which everywhere else had established despotism.

The political history of the northern kingdoms is no less remarkable.

Feudalism never had much strength in Sweden, but this was through conditions very different from those prevailing in commercial countries, and much more comparable to those in Switzerland. The poverty of the soil and the harshness of the climate were such that men there always preserved something of their primitive independence. The order of burghers (*ordre des bourgeois*) [was] very weak there, but the peasants had representation in the diet when they were slaves in all of Europe. Royal power did not acquire a firm hold because the order of burghers, that is to say, trade, industry, and commercial wealth, which emancipated the kings in all countries, were always weak there. The kings, whose only constant support was the bourgeoisie, had merely a ceaselessly fluctuating authority, for it lacked a solid basis and was sustained only by the military talents of a few monarchs.

In Denmark, which is a kind of archipelago situated at the entrance of the Baltic Sea, the influence of industry was necessarily much more precocious and much greater. Thus for a very long time royal power has been better established there than in Sweden, and has finally become absolute.

Norway is a country too weak to have an independent genius. After the long quarrels and innumerable revolutions that have disturbed Scandinavia, it remains subject to the king of Denmark, though Sweden has a much more formidable basis of military power. This is another proof that the energy of power has always been greater in Denmark.

I will say nothing of Russia. This state, which seems to be compounded of feudalism, northern barbarism, and oriental government, cannot be judged on the same principles as European governments. To investigate it in depth would require a study much more difficult than advantageous.

The king of Prussia was not long ago an aristocrat of the Germanic realm. His acquisitions, resulting in large part from the force of arms, contributed, together with the situation of his states, to favor the direct movement from feudal government to military despotism.

Such also, although more slowly, was the development of all the states of the house of Austria. The progress of wealth, slow in inland states, nevertheless gradually comes to serve royal power by giving it the means to raise taxes, and will probably never lead the people to amount to anything politically. The immense military resources which these regions contain will belong increasingly to the monarch, to the extent that he possesses the means to pay for them, and less to the nobility, led by the growth of luxury to exchange their power for pleasures. Despotism will not cease . . .

It is probable that in time these despotic states of inland Europe will dominate and assimilate the aristocratic states. Already for a number of years these alliances for acquisition among natural enemies . . .[3]

By reviewing the small inland states ruled in a monarchical form I could prove that the same cause has acted with the same regularity; but these details are unnecessary and would only serve to confuse. Moreover, as states become more powerful, the less their inner mode of existence depends on external [political] influences, the more they are themselves and consequently suitable for observing the influence [of physiography].

[2. *Maritime States*]

I turn to the monarchies whose geographical situation on the sea, combined with a temperate climate, seems to allow commercial wealth and the resulting popular power the greatest development.

Let us leave aside the kingdoms of Naples and Sicily. These countries, endlessly disputed by the first powers of Europe, have depended for their political existence on foreign influence. I

---

3. Barnave refers to the first partition of Poland and to the second, which was imminent or possibly under way as he wrote.

will not stop at Portugal. It is above all necessary to examine Spain, England, and France.

The history of Spain is striking. This region is one of the most fortunately situated for commerce and navigation, and democratic power was to make great progress there. Furthermore, despite the warfare of Christians and Moors which so long held them back, manufactures, the arts, and the power of the towns were more precocious there than in any other of the European monarchies. From the fourteenth and fifteenth centuries, the industry and power of the towns equalled and surpassed the influence of the aristocracy in most of Spain. Monarchical unity, established under Ferdinand and Isabella, doubtless owed much to this secret principle, as a result of the aid that clever prince knew how to derive from it. This second stage of the monarchy would soon have been followed by a [third] in which its [constitution] was organized. The rapid progress of popular power and the noble character of the Spanish nation would have denied despotism the time to establish itself had not the discovery of the New World intervened to alter the relation between people and prince and reverse the destiny of the monarchy.

A commercial nation, educated and civilized, which discovers new regions will establish truly useful relations with them and will derive from this source an increase of its commerce and industry. At the time the Spaniards discovered America they had not arrived at that level of science and politics: full of chivalric and religious ideas, regarding gold as the only wealth, they did not deal with the [conquered] country as [would] a commercial and manufacturing nation, but as ambitious conquerors and intolerant fanatics. Two principal consequences resulted from this event and reacted on the political system of Spain.

The first was that the nation, instead of drawing from this discovery new resources for its commerce and industry and consequently for its wealth and population, was led by false glory and exaggerated hopes of riches to abandon its arts and useful enterprises in order to lose itself [in the New World]. Thus the two elements which make up democratic power, industrial wealth and population, were destroyed by a factor which at another time would have served to strengthen them.

The second effect was that at the moment when the other European princes, seeing their needs increase and the old sources of revenue dry up, became dependent on the commons through the necessity of obtaining subsidies from them, the kings of Spain, enriched by the tribute and the mines of the New World, freed themselves completely from their subjects.

Thus through a great fortuitous circumstance popular power retrogressed, royal power was aggrandized, and all relations were changed. Philip II's deep-rooted and detestable policy—that of a prince who, without need of his subjects' wealth, impoverished and debased in order to subjugate them—supported the natural effect of despotism, which is . . . in its repression. [Thus], one of the most industrious, noble, valiant nations in the world, degraded by an event which seemingly should have raised it to the pinnacle of glory, arrived at old age without having passed through manhood.

England is the most happily situated European country for navigation and for all the branches of industry it sustains. She can be attacked by sea, and there she must defend herself. Transportation between the different points on her coast and all the surrounding islands is by sea. Her shipping comes from her daily needs, and what other peoples possess only through luxury or ambition she had to acquire by necessity. But England is separate from the rest of Europe: in a state of advanced civilization she reaches all points of the world with her vessels; in a state of weak civilization she is in some sense secluded from it. Thus the history of England, one of the Western countries where the establishment of industry and the arts was most difficult, was the one where, once introduced, they made the greatest and most rapid progress.

The history of England has been written by the best modern historian, and her constitution, together with the elements that established it, have been expounded by the most profound political writer since Montesquieu.[4] However, I cannot forbear to sketch a few ideas about this almost exhausted subject. No proof is a more powerful support of the principles I have posed than the political history of England.

It is true that the energy of power established by the Conquest and the distribution of fiefs made by the Conqueror constitute an accidental element which has acted powerfully on England's political destinies. However, I am far from thinking that it influenced them as much as her geographical situation.

England, like the other empires of Europe, has had her feudal anarchy. If the great fiefs had less power and extent there than in France, if the state preserved its unity better, the most natural reasons are: first, the extent of the territory, which allowed the monarchy more means of action and offered less of a basis for the aristocracy; second, the sea . . .; third, the city of London, which, being both a political town and a great seaport, has always had an excessive population and power in proportion to the size of the empire, and has contributed greatly to maintaining its unity.

The energy of monarchical power in the period from Henry VIII to James I, when it was almost without any help of armed force, proves how much England is constituted for unity.

The kings of England, like all others, weakened the aristocracy through the help of the commons. They were absolute until the commons had acquired enough strength to share in the domination they had given them; and as a result of the geographical situation this epoch arrived earlier than in any other monarchy.

The nation having been democratized and fused in a single element, the whole representation was united in one chamber, the House of Lords, that type of legislative and judicial senate of feudal times.

From this resulted a constitution which is certainly the best and most solid that has ever existed in an insular country, but

---

4. According to Rude, *Barnave,* p. 45n., Hume and J.-L. de Lolme, respectively.

whose application to a territorial empire would be of extremely doubtful success. In a territorial empire, a chamber of hereditary nobles would subjugate the people and the king.

The aristocracy is naturally weak in England; and the people on the other hand, are very strong because of industrial wealth; and the monarchy has great energy as a result of the great strength of unity. [For these reasons] in England the House of Lords must always be on the defensive; its hereditary nature gives it only enough power to exist, but also gives it the conservatism and permanence of principles [that strengthens governments].

Whatever natural strength the monarchical principle receives from England's necessary unity, since the king has no army, the dominant power in that country is incontestably the commons. Such is this power that without the considerable means of influence afforded the government by the present system of elections, I doubt that it [the commons] would allow the constitution to exist for long. If those in England who want reform of representation are, as they say, enemies of a change in the basis of the constitution, it may well be that their desires are contradictory. Not having observed the situation at first hand I am not sure but that I may be badly informed on what takes place in England; but if it is true that the ministerial majority exists not so much as the expression of a certain power as of a certain way of administering, that it is so restrained by public opinion and by the interest of preserving its own importance that it would detach itself from the minister the moment he attacked the constitution; if it is true that the oft-cited corruption is not the infamous . . . for gold which dissolves . . . but the distribution of employments, without which no government can proceed; in a word, if such is the existing arrangement that it solves the great problem of political institutions and renders the constitution stable and the government active, it is indeed unfortunate that the rights of a section of representatives are injured by such an order of things, for there are the strongest probabilities that the slightest changes will destroy all its effects.

France, situated between two seas, placed so to speak at the center of commercial Europe, was destined to attain a high degree of industry and commercial wealth; but the great size of its lands strengthened the aristocracy's preponderance for a long time. When the darkness of feudal anarchy began to lift she saw herself divided into great fiefs. Since royal authority could have no sway over so great an area, some strong lords had made local conquests and had become powers. Armed with a consistent policy and the help of the commons, the kings gradually absorbed the great fiefs. If they no longer saw among their subjects princes as powerful as themselves, they still had to struggle with the nobles [and] their leagues. The institution of regular troops under Charles VII, and the policy—deep-laid, perfidious, and harsh—of Louis XI his son, began to win a decided superiority for royal power. This continued until these minorities following the unforeseen death of Henry II. Then the weakness of the government and the stirring of new religious ideas troubled the state for [more than thirty] years. These conditions gave the aristocracy, which still had deep roots, the means to raise itself up once again. Although one of the accidental causes of these troubles was the introduction of the Calvinist sect, whose spirit was entirely democratic, the aristocracy dominated alone; and this demonstrates the force of the principles expressed in this work; [for the aristocracy] dominated not only during the civil wars, but during the troubles of the minorities of Louis XIII and Louis XIV. At the same time in England the absolute power of the Tudors was already confronted with the problem of curbing the democracy. [This] democracy overturned, and restored the Stuarts, and has been, ever since the sixteenth century, the principle of all change and the main force of the state.

Henry IV, a great warrior and an even greater politician, who had the instinct of power and knew how to surround it with magic—who had the three characteristics by which kings become absolute: economy, force, and seduction—reconquered the throne and would have reestablished royal authority, had he lived!

Cardinal Richelieu took up his work. Louis XIII allowed

power to a [minister] rather through reason than weakness, which is a rare thing. Gifted with equally energetic genius and character, this minister succeeded in liberating the crown from the tutelage of the nobility and reduced the last great lords.

Since his time the aristocracy, which struggled alone against the throne until the middle of the eighteenth century, has existed only in corporations, noble bodies, provincial estates, the clergy, the judicial bodies.

The judicial bodies, created by the king and dependent on him, had been the principal instrument of the aggrandizement of his power; they also contributed to its decadence. The Parlement of Paris, which descended from the old feudal court, included peers. Our princes, who did not want to assemble the Estates General, allowed the parlements to acquire a certain confidence.

Finding it difficult to raise money, they established the venality of offices, and the magistracy thus became independent. It had been bourgeois and royalist; it became noble, feudal, refractory. There resulted a combination extremely unfavorable to power, that in which the judicial order is in opposition to it; for then it has to oppose the force which should support it, and is obliged to replace it by irregular means, which are always more offensive than efficacious and lead to the greatest abuses—annulments of judgments, extraordinary tribunals, commissions, *lettres de cachet.*

Popular strength increasing steadily as the aristocracy declined, the democratic explosion took place at the end of the eighteenth century. It is not part of the subject of this discourse to develop the particular causes that hastened and strengthened it.

The highest period of royal power was under Elizabeth in England, and in France under Louis XIV.

The democratic explosion in England preceded that in France by a hundred and fifty years.

Because of the difference in the times the ferment of opinion that sustained democratic power in England was the passion of religious reform; in France the passion of philosophizing (*philosophisme*)—the former made the impetus more violent, the latter chiefly weakened the obstacles.

But I shall trace elsewhere the parallel of these two revolutions. I have tried here to indicate the general development that dominates European governments and has led us to the violent upheaval we have just experienced. It is time to examine the immediate causes that determined it and to pursue it in detail.

Chapter XII

[Immediate Causes Which Occasioned the French Revolution]

The democratic principle, almost stifled in all European governments as long as the feudal regime remained vigorous, has since that time unceasingly gathered strength and moved toward its fulfillment.

While the arts, commerce, and luxury enriched the industrious section of the people, impoverished the large landed proprietors, and brought the classes closer together in wealth, the sciences and education brought them closer in morals and recalled men to primitive ideas of equality.

Joined almost everywhere with these natural conditions was the influence of royal power. Long oppressed by the aristocracy, it called the people to its aid. For a long time the people serve as the throne's auxiliary against their common enemies; but when they have acquired enough strength no longer to [accept] a subordinate role, they burst forth and take their place in the government.

Various causes may hasten or delay this natural advance; but the most powerful is certainly the geographic situation of different lands. The more their position favors commerce and navigation, the more they are assimilated to the rest of the world and the sooner democratic power will develop there. The more this situation isolates them, binds them to agricultural work, and exposes them to the fury of war, the later the people become aware of their strength and learn their rights.

When the unfortunate Louis XVI ascended the throne, everything in France was ready for a democratic revolution, and the conduct of the government actively promoted it.

Cardinal Richelieu had succeeded in humbling the aristocracy, resurgent during the civil wars. Louis XIV, heir to absolute power, untroubled save for a moment by the tumults of the regency, sustained and consolidated it by the admiration . . . and even more by the ascendancy of a domineering character.

After him began the succession of idler kings. But power was still young: it had passed from him with so much [authority] and energy that neither the sudden caprices of the regent nor the laxity and scandals of Louis XV could shake it.

Moreover if the government of these two men was without virtue, it was not without cleverness. Louis XIV had aggrandized power in order to chain a nation still bold and noble; they debased the nation in order to subjugate it to a power already degraded. They destroyed obstacles, debased morals, seemed to want to destroy the very springs of pride and honor, putting financial success above birth and creating a thousand shameful ways to attain wealth. They aimed at the kind of equality that makes the security of despotic governments.

Even the progress of education, which was one day to destroy despotism, seemed to serve it. The seventeenth century had been one of imagination; with it disappeared those exalted sentiments, those brilliant fictions which for a time sustained the national character against the efforts of an absolute government. [But in the eighteenth century] literature and the arts took on the tones of the [prevailing] morality and followed the direction of the government.

Philosophy, which steadily gained momentum, threw itself [into the attack on superstition]; but while it was allowed its position on superstition, it agreed to continue to respect the throne. It was even seen prostituting itself to . . . and men who since . . . Finally, such was the success of this thoroughgoing system of degradation that the nation no longer knew anything but love of gold, the attraction of pleasure, and the most frivolous vanity; and when it was put to the test by the violent acts that signalled the end of this reign, it united so much obedience with so much contempt for its master that it seemed ready to tolerate anything.

But the existing government had nevertheless reached the time of its maturity. Deprived of the bonds of respect and affection, it continued to rule, so to speak, only by mechanical means. The two privileged orders which still formed the machinery of government had ruined themselves in their luxury and debased themselves morally. The third estate, on the contrary, had acquired extensive enlightenment and immense wealth. The nation was held in check only by its habituation to slavery and its sense of the impossibility of breaking its chains. But [new] opinion[s], which the government still curbed, had made immense progress in the depth of the nation, and already in the rising generation the precepts of Helvétius and Rousseau began to cause Voltaire's to be forgotten.

For royal authority to sustain itself in such circumstances would have required that the throne be occupied by a tyrant or a great man. Tiberius would have preserved his power in achieving the [subjugation] and degradation of his people; Charlemagne would have maintained his ascendancy by summoning them to reforms of which he himself would have been the leader, arbiter, and moderator.

Louis XVI was neither one nor the other. He was too virtuous not to try to correct the abuses he had been scandalized to observe; [but] he had neither the character nor the talents which could have restrained an impetuous nation whose actual condition and [whose] monarch['s ideas] summoned it to reform.

His reign was a succession of attempts for the good, acts of weakness and ineptitude.

If there was a way of preventing the explosion of popular power, it would have been to associate it with the established government [and] open all careers to the third estate. The contrary was done: because a corrupt government had broken the power of the aristocracy, it was believed that a paternalistic government must reestablish it. The parlements were recalled, birth was once again accorded all its advantages, the third estate was more and more excluded from military careers. Laws were established which were opposed to existing morals, to the natural course of things: everything was done to arouse the jealousy of one class and exalt the pretensions of the other. The third estate became accustomed to see in the throne a hostile power which it alone could support or overturn. The aristocrats were allowed that intoxication which, afterward, when [the government] tried to strike them down, led them to provoke a revolution of which they became the victims.

The council's procedures and the court's conduct outdid each other in pushing the nation toward innovations and in destroying the ancient prestige of authority.

A series of innovating ministers, attempting but not accomplishing a thousand reforms, accustomed the nation to the idea of amelioration without . . .

A court in which . . . unforeseeing youth had succeeded the profound corruption of Louis XV's courtiers made a game of abolishing all customs, of . . .

What the nature of things had prepared [and] the conduct of the government had [encouraged] was provoked by the American war. Through that miraculous linkage of circumstances which produces extraordinary events, while everything was making [for domestic troubles], external policy, on its part, tended to bring about the revolution of France and perhaps hasten that of Europe.

The authors of this political system, in allying France with Austria, had the object of maintaining peace on the Continent, of devoting all our surplus wealth to the growth of our shipping, the humbling of England, and the increase of our commerce. Following the same ideas they had prepared and fomented the insurrection of the English colonies against their metropolis. When [this insurrection] matured it had to be supported. Hence the war, resulting in three consequences which favored our revolution: the first, that the nation was filled with ideas of insurrection and liberty; the second, that the army, already assimilated to the civilian population by a long peace, [was influenced by the new ideas] and joined the enthusiasm of civic to soldierly virtues; the third, that the [government's] finances were completely [ruined]. Thus while the government was faced with a public opinion threatening to its very existence, the two principal instruments of power suddenly crumbled in its hands.

However, it had regained some reputation. To the success of its arms and its negotiations were joined the popularity of a minister[5] clever in surrounding himself . . . and if at that time there had been the courage to examine candidly the state of [public] finances and to [deal with it] by immense reforms, postponing the hour of necessity and maintaining its [the government's] control over public opinion, it could have directed the changes which had become necessary in government . . . and would have softened the shock.

But the evil was not sufficiently recognized for so painful a remedy to be accepted. The court was far from consenting to it, and the minister, far from attempting it, was quite incapable of any firm resolution. He had lacked the courage to impose his ideas on the nation during the war, nor did he have enough to demand adequate reforms from the king. He wanted to please, he concealed the evil, he accepted a kind of system which was the combined effect of the practices of his calling and the dominant disposition of his character. He based finances on credit and credit on the moral character of the minister of finance. In making himself thus necessary, he doubtless hoped to mend parts of the machinery and remedy the evil before it was known. He was not given even time to devote himself to these feeble palliatives. He carried with him the regrets of a nation which rendered justice to his probity and exaggerated his talents.

One who suffers from a profound malady and lacks even the

---

5. Jacques Necker, the Genevan banker, who was Directeur-Général des Finances from 1776 to 1781.

very resolution to endure any regimen calls empirics to his aid. This is what was done then. There appeared that man whose name will be linked to the memory of the French Revolution as its evil genius.[6] Far from there being a question of economy under his administration, he was prodigal by character, complaisance, and system. Just as a ruined man tries to dazzle by his ostentation, hoping for some unexpected resource in the kind of esteem he attracts, so this minister seemed to want to win over powerful men by his lavishness and to intoxicate the nation by a factitious prosperity. [Thus he hoped] to prepare everything and to be master of opinion at the moment when he would reveal the bold measures by which he imagined he would [restore the finances].

He finally brought on that famous time when the deficit was revealed and when statesmen could foresee almost everything that has happened since.

Some of the things he proposed might have succeeded, had they been presented by a respected minister after extensive reforms in expenditure, and when needs were not as large nor as pressing. But when a discredited government, scandalous in its lavishness, suddenly reveals its extreme distress, enjoying neither respect nor fear, all its proposals seem to be snares and its demands arouse only indignation and contempt.

What it could not obtain through confidence it proposed to exact by authority. Then began a struggle which, until the convocation of the Estates General, offered only the spectacle of the death throes of power. The more its means were destroyed, the more violent became its efforts.

Finally the Estates General assembled at Versailles. In order to judge succeeding events well it is necessary above all to form a correct idea of the state of affairs and of the respective dispositions of all [those] whose combined influence was to act on the Revolution.

6. C.-A. de Calonne, who was Controleur-Général des Finances from 1783 to April 1787.

Chapter XIII

[Combined Influences Which Were to Act on the Revolution]

The commons on the one hand and the privileged orders on the other arrived ready for conflict, and their quarrels were to begin over the very forms of deliberation. The nobility and the clergy, united in the double intention of winning as much as they could from the throne and giving to the people the least possible, were strongly attached to the forms of 1614. These forms, which gave each order the right of deliberating separately and of opposing its veto to the propositions of the other two orders, guaranteed the preservation of their privileges and gave them a means, by showing those close to the throne the usefulness of their vote, of obtaining advantageous concessions. The commons, without holding fixed ideas, having nevertheless as their principal object to weaken the privileges and reconquer the usurpations of the first orders, held strongly to deliberation by head. And since in these two forms of deliberation some saw all their possibilities of self-preservation, others all their hopes of advancement—since the first had on their side established usage, the others natural reason—these debates would have been interminable had they not been resolved either by the intercession of the government or by the power of the people.

Now let us examine the situation of these two powers, one newly born and the other close to death.

Several provinces had already been given over to a prolonged agitation when the bailliage assemblies and the composition of the cahiers stirred all minds, occupied the different classes with contrary claims, filled the third estate with hopes, and gave it awareness of its power.

Natural or artificial causes, having produced a great shortage

INTRODUCTION TO THE FRENCH REVOLUTION   129

of necessities at the time, resulted in popular disturbances in several towns.

Finally the capital, whose immense population was to have such a large influence on events, already agitated by the elections and by the different writings with which all regions had inundated it, contained two further sources of ferment which, although operating more covertly, were not less active. One was that secret war which Europe's two great leagues continued to wage in the midst of an apparent peace. France and her allies, having prepared and effected the schism of the English colonies, had encouraged the first attempts at a revolution in Holland, which, in changing the form of her government, were to cause a change in her external relations. Meanwhile, the enemy powers, skillful in avenging themselves by the same means, nurtured the seeds of trouble in France and Brabant. The kings, forgetting the common dangers, prepared . . .

The other . . .

All these circumstances indicated that if the debates were prolonged, if they caused public anxiety and the paralysis of power to continue, the people would intervene to end [the discussions] and, once master [of the situation], could become the mover and arbiter of events.

The government by itself could have [controlled events] by anticipating them with a prudent steadfastness. Here is how things stood with it.

The court and the ministry were divided into two principal groups. One was that of the princes, extravagant chiefs of a faction which had been encouraged only by their support. Thenceforward secretly directed by the one[7] who has since become the . . . of their errors, incapable of judging the situation, they openly supported the aristocratic cause, and their object was much less to prevent the fall of authority than to claim a large personal influence in the administration of affairs.

---

7. The princes were the king's brothers, the Comte de Provence and the Comte d'Artois. By the "one" who "secretly directed," Barnave probably referred to Calonne, who became the chief adviser of the Comte d'Artois, rallying point of the diehard émigrés.

The other group had for its chief the minister of finance;[8] his great popularity was its main support. With it were connected a part of the ministry and the small number of persons at court who had been attached to the popular cause. Through the clouds and vacillations that always enveloped this minister's intentions, it seemed that he inclined toward a system of government somewhat similar to England's. But there is reason to believe that he had by no means studied the existing situation.

If the government, cutting short the debates that arose between the orders, had come to the aid of the commons before they became aware of all their power; if from the first days its influence had persuaded the orders to deliberate in common, it probably would have gained a great [influence] over the resolutions; if, in keeping with the then prevailing disposition of the deputies, the work had been done in much less time; if, anticipating the violent convulsions to which succeeding events delivered the kingdom, the work of the assembly had not been continuously influenced by the inflammatory atmosphere of a people in a state of revolution; if all the ancient elements of the body social, working in concert to give it a new form, had not been divided by open hatreds and had still seemed invested with their respective powers, the result would have been some kind of compromise among the various elements, a new arrangement of what existed rather than a complete transformation.

But the only one who could have done this lacked the means in his character, and perhaps in his position; far from adopting this open and resolute course, the government seemed to hope that the prolonged debates of the three orders would reduce them to turning to it. It even believed perhaps that the credit of the Estates General with the nation would sink, that public opinion, tired of so much discussion, rallying to [the government], would invest it with sufficient credit to become the supreme arbiter of all it undertook.

These frivolous speculations soon vanished. What could have

---

8. Necker, who had returned to the government in August 1788.

been done by the government was done without it and against it. The commons, wearied of such [slowness] and sensing that they were supported by public opinion, declared in constituting themselves that they represented the nation; and thenceforward they were the sole power. From that moment the fate of the Revolution was almost completely decided.

At least it was decided in opinion, and was soon to be so in fact. The legal authority, which had not known how to forestall this great step, undertook to oppose it. Irresolute when action was necessary, it became violent when nothing remained for it but to give in. The royal session [June 23, 1789] was to show it the inflexible courage of the commons; led . . .

Appendix
Selections from
Barnave's Notebooks[1]

1. [Of the Moral Sciences Among the Ancients and the Moderns]

The ancient philosophers dealt with general physics (*haute physique*) purely by theory.

But of the science of ethics and of all that related directly to man, such as legislation, they made a factual science, founded on experience and observation; they seemed to believe that in matters so closely bound to happiness one could not rely on theoretical reasoning.

Modern philosophers have followed an opposite course. They have illuminated general physics by the most positive methods of observation, experiment, and calculation; but as to ethical and political science, they have thought that metaphysical generalities were good enough. We have the social contract instead of all the positive ideas of the Greek political writers, and for us the definitions of Helvétius take the place of the maxims of Socrates.

---

1. The twelve numbers below refer to the selections in this Appendix, and the references in parentheses to the volumes and page numbers where they may be found in Bérenger's *Oeuvres de Barnave* (see p. 1, n. 1). The editor reproduced these selections with a rough accuracy, although with deletions and additions which he did not indicate, and which I have for the most part corrected: 1 (III, 1–2); 2 (III, 2–4); 3 (III, 10–13); 4 (III, 29–30); 5 (IV, 101–103); 6 (IV, 267–71); 7 (I, 148); 8 (I, 184–85); 9 (II, 137–42); 10 (II, 150); 11 (II, 152–57); 12 (II, 157–60).

2. [Of the Errors of Men and Peoples]

Rarely do men deceive themselves in the notions that result from daily practice and observation.

But it is rare that they are not deceived in theories which are the work of imagination and reasoning.

Thus nothing is more misleading than the prejudices or opinions accepted in almost all the speculative (*sublimes*) sciences [and] which preoccupy their adepts. But nothing is more generally true than the prejudices or the ideas which have been formed about the particularities of living, about ethics, about man's practical knowledge.

The more naïve (*neufs*) and closer to their origins peoples are, the more absurd their large theories and the truer their practical notions. The more they advance in their civilization, the more their theories are purified and their practical notions corrupted.

The philosophy of naïve peoples is wisdom; that of highly civilized peoples (*peuples vieillis*) is metaphysics. Among the first the multitude has a highly developed instinct, and their wise men do hardly more than perfect this instinct and reduce it to maxims. Among the latter, the multitude has no more than a limited and depraved instinct, and wise men occupy themselves with abstract sciences which have almost nothing in common with the practice of life.

It seems to me that since the early philosophers and poets of Greece, the knowledge of moral man has lost more than it gained. It may be that since Hippocrates practical medicine has made no further progress. A remarkable thing! The ancients were ignorant of the circulation of the blood and of most of the notions of chemistry, and [yet] with no more than the knowledge afforded by direct observation they had better medical men than we.

But if they equalled or surpassed us in the sciences and arts resulting from direct observation, sensation, and instinct, such as ethics, medicine, poetry, and several of the fine arts, we have greatly surpassed them in those complicated and, so to speak, abstract arts *(hors de la nature)* which result from the application of a general theory *(haute théorie)*, [such as] navigation, mechanics and all its applications, chemistry, etc.

3. [*Right and Fact*]

It is a frequent source of errors and disputes among men not to distinguish precisely right from fact.

Right is that which results from positive laws or from maxims of justice derived from the nature of man and from his natural and social interests.

Fact is what observation and experience have demonstrated actually to exist, or at least [to exist] in the ordinary course of things.

Empirical minds give their principal attention to fact; they acquire an extensive knowledge of the course of nature. In their work for the happiness of man they set aside what is impossible, they strive to attain for humanity, or rather for the part with which they are concerned, the degree of perfection and the kind of felicity of which they deem it capable.

Speculative minds are hardly concerned with anything but right. They condemn everything which does not conform to their own ideas of ethics and justice. They exist almost always amid either illusions and chimerical hopes or in indignation against reality. The first [empirical minds] usually accuse the others of ignorance, weakness of mind, puerile delusions.

The latter in their turn accuse [their adversaries] of immorality, since they mistake their assertions for their principles; and also of paradox since, accustomed to view nature through their dreams, they no longer recognize it when it is shown to them as it is.

People who have formed illusions abandon everything when these are dissipated; they have worked for a chimerical good which disappears. A real or possible good holds no charm for them. They fall into the contrary extreme, and seeing that the humanity for which they destined the happiness and perfection of angels cannot rise to the value of their benefits, they wish upon it all kinds of shame and evil.

The weakness of empirical minds is also to draw excessively harsh conclusions from the vices and imperfections of man; either, exaggerating these things, they destine man to a treatment in accordance with the exaggeratedly low and odious idea they have formed; or they decide simply to let man go on as he will. The first have arrived through the study of reality at a kind of misanthropy, the others at unconcern. *Hobbes* was in the first group; *Montaigne* was not far from the second.

However, nature, such as it is, is still inexhaustible in resources and rich in perfectibility. It is only necessary to know well what she is, what she can be, and by what route she can arrive at that point. Science needs a sagacious spirit and a cool head. Art needs a bold character, an ardent soul, a fertile imagination, illumined by the same intelligence which has been capable of discovering truth. It is necessary to know and to will. Unfortunately nature has rarely combined these things, and a calm, sound judgment is not ordinarily the lot of an energetic and resourceful spirit.

In the moral sciences there are speculative or empirical minds, some concerned with right, others with fact. Similarly, in the physical sciences one finds men of theory and men who experiment with reality, the first seeking to explain nature, the others to discover the system of nature by gathering facts.

4. *Of Reason*

Some limited minds, claiming exclusive title to rationality because they are incapable of anything more, have given reason such a bad reputation that almost all people of true intelligence have ceased to care about it. They fly from it as from the most dangerous hazard to genius, to amiability, to pleasure. They are wrong. Reason is the gift of appreciating everything, of assigning to everything its value, its place, its use, according to nature and not according to the narrow ideas of beings who claim to be its exclusive possessors. Far from hindering reason, wit and imagination serve it in offering a greater number of grounds for its application *(motifs pour se déterminer)*, aiding and illuminating it through a thousand new discoveries concerning the character of men, insights into their hearts, and the customs of the societies where one is placed. Reason may be called the art of choosing well. If she senses that everything is weighed at her tribunal, she sometimes forbids its appearance, and according to circumstances she takes on an unreasonable bearing. Reason does not tell us: be tranquil, moderate, frugal, sparing; she tells us: be what probity, your tastes, [and] society prescribe that you be. She commands one person to be modest and tranquil, another to be ambitious, active; but [in both cases] she desires the most certain and rapid methods, those most appropriate to arriving at the goal. She shows them to each individual, she combines them according to his faculties, his qualities, with the circumstances. She prescribes, in turn, patience, steadfastness, address, boldness, activity.

5. *Influence of the Philosophical Sect on Literature in General*

The philosophical sect of our time has been marked by pedantry, contemptuous arrogance, insensibility of heart, abuse of theory, the reforming and innovating spirit without investigation, without adequate ideas.

Observing the prejudices of men, the obscurity of the sources of their knowledge, [the *philosophes*] have treated everything as prejudice; they have completely overturned the authority of opinion.

They have constantly urged the observation of nature, and have constantly gone astray on false paths because of the inadequacy of their observation—an almost inevitable abuse in speculative studies. They constantly reexamined their ideas; but what they knew furnished too little nourishment for the work of intelligence.

To think instead of learning; to believe in nothing, to judge according to oneself, this was our course; and then, enthusiasm, deviations, vices; all the excesses of this spirit spread out into society; young people especially welcomed and exaggerated it; influences good and bad appeared in multiplicity, a variety of forms which would require a large book to describe.

The same men were possessed of dialectic, order, precision, scope, vigor of abstraction, and all the other advantages of a sound metaphysics.

Society received from them a new language as well as a new temper. Expression became precise, cold, free, according to circumstances. There resulted a special pedantry, innovations in language, in metaphysical usages.

Many errors were reformed, there was less credulity; there were considerably fewer objects [of discussion], and these were much more thoroughly reasoned.

Amid this ignorance, this liberty of opinion, this speculative tendency, the weakness of hearts and of heads led men into numerous and bizarre deviations; thus (1) systems of every kind increased without limit; (2) there were born all those metaphysical follies of magnetism, of Martinism, of religious enthusiasms.

Ages of ignorance create palpable prejudices; ages of sophistry create metaphysical deviations.

The didactic, analytic spirit has placed itself where it ought least to be. Tragic heroes have become philosophers, passions are expressed by maxims. Poetry, nourished by metaphysics, is desicated. The language of thought replacing that of the sentiments and feelings has substituted nothing more for their unction and ardor than the brilliance of enthusiasm.

6. *J.–J. Rousseau*

Rousseau ruminated long over his thought, created and fashioned it slowly; his style reflects this effort.

His thoughts and opinions are colored by the influence of an afflicted constitution.

Rousseau has energy, strength of feeling and reasoning, Raynal abundance, Sterne liberty, abandon, the easy and natural flights of heart and head.

Rousseau was born to feel; circumstances led him to reasoning. Generally his ideas are more solid than fine, his impressions more forceful than delicate, his sentiments more violent than soft.

With even less lightness than delicacy, his humor is heavy and reasoned. He knows nothing of the libertinage of mind which lures thought far from [common] sentiment and opinion. Serious, attaching importance to everything, the good and the true roll from his pen, never allowing it to flit along the paths of folly.

Also, even with his enthusiasm, he has no abandon. His work is that of a strong but laborious writer, rapid at times, never carefree and easy. He has exaltation; his character is inconstant, changeable, prone to adopt anything in excess. His mind is eloquent and supple, adept at giving plausibility to anything in his own eyes and others'.

He had no education which would have fixed in him the habit of moderation. On this subject, however, he had a mass of ideas and a lack of reasonableness which delivered his opinion over to any illusion, and his character to any deviation, [and] since they were not formed by early training, he was as defenseless against the incitements of opinion as against the influence of circumstances.

His passions were almost all connected with weakness; his pride was not serene, but reactive. He had a great need of the opinion of others; he took fright easily; anxious and suspicious, he was always complaining or crying out for fear someone might attack him. He was without nobility of character, harsh with the weak . . . His presumption was insolent, and he was in his own way self-satisfied. He was always given to reproaches, groans, or despair about his misfortunes. He was malevolent and loved no one truly. He was meanly ashamed of kindnesses offered or received, and had a strong inclination to ingratitude. In his passions there was an inordinate arrogance and real misanthropy.

His style is rich, full of invention and taste. Served by an admirable sensitivity of ear, mind, and heart, Rousseau added to these an appropriate fertility and suppleness of imagination.

Through his infinite resources of ideas, sophisms and sentiments he had a marvellous talent for seducing the mind and the heart. He could have been an excellent preacher, an excellent lawyer, an irresistible corrupter.

He always wrote in exaltation, often through the night.

Through his writings he encouraged many young girls to err. He spoiled many educations. He greatly influenced the minds of the young and made madmen of people who would have been merely fools, and who, for the rest, perhaps were impelled by him to a movement to which reflection, age, and other studies have since given better direction.

For his part, he accustomed the age to discard prejudices and to delight in paradoxes.

He encouraged sentiment and retarded or weakened the progress of egoism, of callousness and moral baseness, and also of irreligion; for he defended religion with arguments which, although in no way conclusive, were among the few which could succeed in this age. But while supporting it he contributed to the discrediting of its ministers.

He also contributed much to the confusion of all accepted opinions, to the emancipation of young people from old ideas, and to their adoption of bizarre and extreme ones which influenced their conduct, their manners, and their morals.

He gave birth to that new style, compounded of enthusiasm, virtue, and sensual ardor, which has since presided over so many writings and which reigns in so many young heads—that style so suitable for ennobling love and sowing libertinage among those of both sexes who are most sound and most moral; so suitable also perhaps in making [this attitude] more widespread, in rendering it less disastrous and separating it from the vices it entailed or which it formerly took for granted.

7. [Revolution and Morals]

In a nation long nurtured in liberty the citizens have acquired a manly and vigorous character. Accustomed to defending their rights against despotism, they are no less adept in guaranteeing them against the attacks and snares of false apostles of the public good. When these nations are in ferment the masses enter into the public movement, and the legitimate interest and decent passions of the greater number easily subjugate the usurping views and disordered passions of the minority.

It is not the same in a soft and corrupt nation, led by extraordinary circumstances to a revolution for liberty. There the people act in keeping with the disposition acquired in their former condition: the majority and, if it must be said, the sound part of the nation, occupied with its work, takes almost no share in public events, desiring only tranquillity, fearing only change: the revolution is made without its participation. It may approve or obey it, but it does not cooperate. The leaders who, encouraged by circumstances, attempted it, are supported only by an active minority, agitated by passions completely foreign to the public good: in one class by pride and ambition, in others by jealousy and love of pillage.

8. [Commerce and National Interests]

France, summoned by her position as much to commerce and the sea as to continental domination, cannot acquire a free and stable constitution except by taking the first course with renewed energy. And since her resources in men and natural wealth are infinitely superior to England's, she must before long rival and surpass her.

Despite all that has been said by the authors of lofty and noble theories on the advantages derived by nations from the prosperity of other peoples, despite all that is heard in our time about the fraternity of free peoples, it is certain that history gives the lie to these maxims; and whether political prosperity is like power which must be seized, or whether men can appreciate their condition only through its relative rather than absolute advantages, it is certain that nations, like individuals, are mutually jealous of glory and that nowhere is this passion so active as among commercial peoples.

9. *Of the Effect of Commerce on Governments*

Commerce gives rise to a large class, disposed to external peace, internal tranquillity, and attached to the established government.

It creates great fortunes which in republics are the origin of a powerful aristocracy.

In general, by enriching the towns and their inhabitants, by multiplying the class of artisans (*ouvriers*), by making available careers of wealth, independent of birth and of any favor of the prince, it strengthens the democratic element and gives the people and the towns a great influence in government.

[Commerce] achieves the same result by impoverishing the landed proprietors through the new enjoyments it offers them, leading to the transformation of the luxury of *ostentation* and *hospitality* into the luxury of *softness* and *voluptuousness*.

It leads to the use of mercenary troops in place of personal service. It introduces into the whole nation luxury, softness, avarice, as well as work.

The morals of a commercial nation are not completely those of merchants. The merchant is thrifty; general morals are prodigal. The merchant maintains his morals; public morals are dissolute.

The mixture of wealth and enjoyment procured by commerce, together with the liberty of morals, with libertinage, ostentation . . . introduced in the nation by the example of the court and the spirit of the nobility, lead to that excess and dissoluteness of all kinds—and also to that perfection of elegance and taste—which prevailed in Rome, mistress of the world, and in France before the Revolution. Rome, where the wealth which flowed in from the whole world was squandered with all the rashness of ambition, the license of the soldier, the indifference of the patrician—France, where the wealth accumulated by an immense commerce and the various labors of the most industrious nation in the world was expended according to the example of a brilliant and corrupt court, by a prodigal and chivalrous nobility, by a . . . and voluptuary capital.

When a nation is exclusively commercial it can acquire an immense amount of wealth without a palpable decline of its morals. The merchant's passion is avarice and his habit work. Given over to this single instinct, he amasses wealth in order to possess it and hardly knows how to use it. He needs examples to lead him to prodigality, ostentation, to the corruption of morals.

In general the merchant is the opposite of the warrior: the one wants to acquire by industry, the other by conquest; the one makes power a means to wealth, the other, wealth a means to power; the one is disposed to save what comes from his work, the other to squander what comes from his valor; the one sacrifices only to his interests under the appearance of probity; the other, in the midst of brigandage and violence, is at least capable of some candor. The one is much occupied in not being disturbed, the other works ceaselessly to disturb others.

The one is the prototype of what in our modern states is called bourgeois; the other is the prototype of the nobility. But the European nobility, since the internal security of states has been fixed, has also taken on many of the characteristics of the landed proprietors, a role related to that of the warrior in one aspect, but which differs greatly from it from another point of view, and whose economizing and conservative spirit is even more rigorous than that of the merchant. The nobility has acquired a third role, that of the courtier—a type which might seem superficially as adventurous and as prodigal as the warrior, which has the same facility in repairing losses; [in this role he] can borrow knightly fashions, since everything pleasant and brilliant suits his ideas and can be grasped by his refined sensitivity. But beneath this surface he is a composite of the lowest vices. From this mixture of three elements, variously combined according to periods, classes, and individuals, was formed the character of the French nobility before the Revolution.

However, wealth ends by swelling the heart of the merchant. Faithful for his own part to his tastes and habits, he conceives other views for his children and gives them a different education.

If there is nothing higher in the state than commerce and wealth, the merchant, with no more to desire in private life, dreams of dominating public affairs, and there appears a bourgeois aristocracy!

If the state has a king and a nobility, the merchant, saturated with money, rejects the class where he acquires it in order to attempt to rise to that of honors and power. He makes great sacrifices to obtain for his children an ambiguous position among nobles and courtiers.

The more the wealth of the state comes from commerce, the more its power is in the fleet and the closer the merchant is to governing the state; the more the wealth of the state comes from land [the more] its power is in the army, [and the] closer the nobleman is to the government.

In modern monarchies it is the power of these two classes that shapes the aristocracy and democracy. Commerce, which in certain republics forms an aristocracy or *rather an aristocratized segment of the democracy,* is never anything but democracy in our feudal kingdoms. But two other principles of power have gradually intruded there, which are related less to the nature of things than to events, and which it is very important to take into account. These [derive from] the Church and the legal profession.

10. *Of Taxation*

Among a free people possessing a representative form of government, taxation is usually much greater, better distributed, and always better employed.

Despotism destroys all public resources, pillages individual properties; but far from enlarging the quota of taxation, it never dares assess as much as a represented people could easily pay.

[Taxation] spares either the nobles or the people, depending on the region and the particular form of government.

Of all governments pure aristocracy levies the least taxes, since it is both the most odious and the most fragile.

Despotism generally distributes [taxes] badly because it must be careful of the interests of a few and of the imagination of all. Even if it desires to, [despotism] dares not establish and distribute [them] properly. Customs, monopolies, incidental fees, etc., kinds of taxes that affect men only as individuals are much more convenient for it than regular taxes which affect a whole people simultaneously and in the same form.

In representative governments, when the aristocracy dominates, taxes are levied on the consumption of necessities, that is to say, on the lower class (*petit peuple*): the aristocracy governs and is not timid in such a situation.

Pure aristocracy may reach such a degree of timidity that taxes bear principally on the wealthy. The excess of evil always has some compensation: in this government the pride of the people is provided for in its condition, and its avarice in taxation. I have in mind the aristocracy which governs the people of the towns, the only ones who must be respected, since they are the only ones feared.

In most societies at the time of their origins a part of the land is reserved for the expenses of the fisc. This is the source of a number of aspects of government, whether in the power or the corruption of this institution. It is in certain respects the origin of the domain, it is the origin of benefices, it is in part the origin of fiefs. This usage tends to make the government independent of the people; it weakens the bond of hierarchy among the depositaries of power.

Revenue derived from taxation tends to build the influence of the people and the power of the central government. In general, the indirect tax is related more to power, and the direct tax to liberty: the one may seem a right of the government, the other is always an attribute of the people; the one is more naturally based on force, and the other on the will of the people; the one is more easily disguised with respect to its nature and its product; the other is always apparent.

Indirect taxation flows most naturally to the center and tends more toward unity of government; direct taxation is related more to the locality and tends rather toward federation.

11. [*Of the Public Debt*]

England does not intend to pay her debt.

What is necessary for the government is that [its] credit be sustained and strengthened, that the interest on money steadily fall, that public wealth continue to expand: then taxes may also be augmented, although at a slower rate; [it is also necessary] that a small but permanent sinking fund should balance, if only partially, new loans which may be necessitated by extraordinary needs.

In a country where credit is solid, it is of small importance that the principal of the debt increases if the interest diminishes.

When the debt of the state is in demand it is never necessary to pay the principal. The interest must be considered as a part of the public obligation.

A débâcle would occur if public prosperity decreased, because the interest on money would rise and the yield of taxes would diminish. It may be confidently affirmed that this eventuality is the only one England has to fear with respect to her debt.

If, through means which may be assumed, although not [realistically] conceived, she succeeded in paying her debt, she would run another danger, the overthrow of her constitution.

No class has more interest and more resources in supporting the established government than the creditors of the state. However poorly-ordered the government, this class will always link its own security with the preservation [of the existing regime]; and if the debt is considerable, all the nation's financiers (*capitalistes*) will be involved in it through the interconnections of their affairs. Moreover, manufacturing and commercial activity being dependent on financiers, [the latter] will carry with them a large part of the people of the towns.

In England these bonds are even more powerful and universal. Since the Bank is the creditor of the government, and almost all the people creditors of the Bank, each citizen owning a banknote has an individual interest in maintaining the existing order.

The system of government borrowing is prodigiously attacked, but in a country where the public wealth can allow it, it is as necessary to the maintenance of power as are treasuries in countries where [borrowing] is impossible. It must be considered that today the basis of governments is money, and that political servitude does not have civil servitude as a basis. The power of kings requires new means for its maintenance.

Of all classes, the most independent is that of the proprietors of titled patrimonial lands. It has little fear of civil disorders, little need of protection [and], if it avoids a very prominent part in [public] discussions, runs almost no risk of spoliation. This kind of property often makes for the dependence of an individual, but the independence of his class taken generally is not thereby affected. . . .

I refer to those who have an interest in the social order through property in any kind of estate or useful industry—[but] doubtless no one is more independent than the man who has nothing.

The artisan (*ouvrier*), the manufacturer, the merchant, the majority of financiers, see their existence endangered if public or political order is disturbed, but none as much as the creditor of the state. The government . . . which offers him a certain security is always sure of his support; he backs everything that can assure peace, power, and continuity.

In France the creditors of the state abandoned the old government because they no longer trusted it, and they turned to the new one because they expected everything from it. Since then they have continued to support it. Because the state as a whole and not any of its parts is their debtor, they must uphold its indivisibility as well as its existence. Landed proprietors will always have inclinations toward a federation: it would reduce the weight of taxes and render each, so to speak, a master in his own house. Commercial interests must recognize that in unity there is greater freedom, scope, and support for their transactions—although the more immediate interests of certain towns and individuals may make them perhaps prefer local authority, which would [better] assure their opulence. With respect to the creditors of the state, they have no choice; they can say literally: unity of the commonwealth (*la république*) or death.

In the Constituent Assembly some persons wanted to divide the debt and the greater part of public taxes among the departments; in some measure this was to decree a federative government, to give the departments the power of the purse, which in modern governments is the main one and the basis of others.

Under the new form of government, which leaves almost no strength to the bonds of unity, it is fortunate that the funds destined to discharge the debts of the state were in large part [otherwise] consumed; for had there not been even the public debt drawing support to the center of the state, it is difficult to imagine where the centripetal force would have been.

Nevertheless, if this bond had not been supported by any other; if it were found more oppressive to the people than powerful; if public prosperity diminished so as to make the weight of taxation crushing, the financiers, ruined or expatriated, being without influence; the debt, far from being a means of maintaining unity, would become a reason to break it. For the landed proprietors, then all-powerful and unchecked by a sufficiently vigorous government, would combine with their natural propensities the interest they would have in freeing themselves from a burden henceforth unbearable.

12. [*Of Governments That Hoard*]

In the present state of Europe it is absolutely impossible to wage war from current revenues; it is necessary therefore to wage it either by means of anticipations on future revenues or by savings made from past revenue—that is to say, through loans or through a treasury.

At this time France wages war from capital (the national properties); this is a unique case; but [this capital] is also, nevertheless, a hoard, formed in truth not by saving, but by extraordinary causes and circumstances.

The option between the two methods, borrowing or saving, depends considerably on the character of princes, but it depends in a more general way on their situation, on the extent, wealth, and power of their states, and on the form of the established government.

Whatever the public wealth, where the nature of the government weakens all confidence, where it can seize upon everything by violence and cannot obtain anything through consent, it must hoard; this is the condition of all the governments of Asia.

Public disturbances and the uncertainty of maintaining order gradually produce the same effect. Henry IV hoarded; the custom formerly of all petty feudal princes was to hoard as much as the poverty of their subjects and the ostentation of their expenditures permitted.

A prince who, because of the instability of his existence and the uncertainty of the securities he can offer, provides no stable basis for credit must hoard, especially if his enterprises, his ambition, [and] his perils are out of all proportion to his revenues and his credit. Such has been, and is even still, the situation of the kings of Prussia.

Aristocratic governments are disposed to hoard because of the mistrust, instability, sparingness, and avarice that characterize them.

Hoarding is sometimes a passion among princes, but much more often a necessity. Few princes save unless they must, and many who need to do not; sometimes the revenues, however severely managed, do not suffice for ordinary expenses. And where, with difficulty, they are made to exceed them, the people's resistance to taxation [as well as] vanity, improvidence, and the taste for pleasures have a daily influence which almost always triumphs over the painful counsels of prudence.

When the practice of hoarding is unnecessary, it is rejected not only by the most natural penchants but by sound considerations of interest.

In a rich and industrious country, where the government is solid and regular, it is unreasonable to hoard. That capital (*capitaux*) which, in circulation, multiplies and reproduces the resources which the government will always find ready to fill its needs, would become inert as a result of hoarding. This would amount to holding back the seeds for the [future] harvests of which it could rightly claim a part. In such a country war is made by borrowing, which the saving of peacetime serves to amortize. Thus none of the capital is withdrawn more than momentarily from its normal circulation.

There are some states which are too poor to allow the government to employ either of these methods, and although expenditures are generally quite small, it is almost impossible for the government to sustain itself except by subsidies from foreign powers.

Index

Agriculture, 21, 83
Alquier, 72n
America, discovery of, 116–117
American Revolution, 125–126. *See also* Revolution
Antiquity, 53, 55, 83–84, 133–135
Antoinette, Marie, 12–13
Aristocracy
 in agricultural society, 78–79
 in antiquity, 83
 decline of, 31, 93, 108–110
 and democracy, 22–28, 85–86
 in Europe, 100–101
 and federation, 105
 in France, 124–125, 128–129
 in inland states, 112–115
 in maritime states, 115–121
 and morals, 66–67
 in pastoral society, 78–79
 principle of, 92, 108
 and taxation, 145
Armed Forces
 in commercial republics, 103, 104–105
 in early societies, 81, 83
 in European society, 102
 organization of, 107–108
 and power, 77
Art, 136
Asia, 84
Austria, 40, 63n
 and France, 125
 and Hungary, 113
 political development of, 115
Authority, within Armed Forces, 107–108

Babeuf, 59
Barbarism, 20
Barnave, Joseph
 on aristocracy and democracy, 22–28
 and eighteenth century culture, 35–44
 in French Revolution, 4–16
 on Marx and Bourgeois Revolution, 56–75
 on modernity and the past, 44–56
 as philosophical historian, 1–4
 and philosophical history, 16–22
 on violence and progress, 28–35
Bergin, T. G., 49n
Berthier, intendant of Paris, 72
Bordeaux, port of, 40
Bossuet, Bishop, 18
Boulainvilliers, 30
Bourgeoisie
 historical development of, 82–83
 and revolution, 1–2, 56–59, 60–62
Bradby, E. D., 4n
Brissot, J. P., 6, 10, 15, 39, 72n
Brissotin, 39–40, 72
Bruhat, Jean, 65
Buzot, 39

Calvinism, 41, 120
Capital, 58
 in aristocracy and democracy, 22n
 in early society, 81
 in government finances, 149–150
 in Rome, 84
Capitalism, 32
Capitalists, 101, 146–147
Carthage, Republic of, 84, 103–104
Cassirer, Ernst, 45n
Catholicism, 95–98. *See also* Clergy
Causality, accidental, 96, 97, 110–111, 118, 120. *See also* Reason
Champ de Mars, massacre of, 12
Chaplier Law, 10
Charlemagne, 124
Charles VII, king of France, 120
China, empire of, 84
Civil society, 66, 68–69, 93, 95
Class struggle, 2, 2n
Clergy, 95, 97–98, 128
Club Massiac, 7, 8
Cobban, Alfred, 60–63

151

Colonialism, French, 6–9
Commerce
  and democracy, 98
  effects of, 141–144
  in Europe, 89, 92
  after French Revolution, 62
  in Greek states, 83
  rise of, 34, 81–82
Committee on Colonies, 6, 7
Comte, Auguste, 45
Condillac, 19, 40
Condorcet, Marquis de, 6, 34, 36, 37, 39, 43, 44, 48
Conquests, effects of, 88–89
Constant, Benjamin, 2n
Constituent Assembly, 8, 9, 14, 61, 61n, 148
Constitution of 1791, 38
Constitutionalism, 11
Courtier, role of nobility, 143–144
Credit, and public debt, 146–150
Crusades, 95, 96

d'Alembert, 54
d'Artois, Comte, 129n
Dauphiné, province of, 1–2, 4, 14, 38
de Broglie, Victor, 5
de Calonne, C.-A., 127, 129n
de la Drôme, Bérenger, 1n, 65n, 75
de Lameth, Alexandre, 5, 6, 7, 9, 15
de Lameth, Charles, 5, 7, 15
de Méréville, Laborde, 5, 39
de Provence, Comte, 129n
Debien, G., 4n
Debts, public, 146–148
Decadence, idea of, 48, 54
Declaration of Rights, 6
Democracy
  and agriculture, 21
  and antiquity, 83–84
  and aristocracy, 22–28
  basis of, 85, 92, 108
  classical, 26
  in commercial republics, 105
  in early societies, 78–79, 82
  in England, 118–119, 120
  in feudalism, 31
  in France, 120–121
  and history, 20, 71
  in Italy and Flemish Republics, 98–101
  moral desirability of, 40–41
  and property, 58
  pure, 101
  and religion, 41–42
Denmark, monarchy of, 114
Despotism, 144–145
  military, 106, 108, 110–115, 117
  in Orient, 84
Diderot, Denis, 70
Duport, Adrien, 5, 6, 9, 15, 38

Eden Treaty of 1786, 63
Education, 85, 123–124
Egret, Jean, 4n
Elizabeth, queen of England, 121
Empirical mind, 135–136
Encyclopédie (1751-65), 35–36
Engels, Friedrich, 22n
England
  and credit, 146–147
  economic rivalries of, 40, 62–63, 141
  and Flemish republics, 99
  political development of, 117–119, 120, 121
Enlightenment, 4, 17
  and development of society, 96
  on feudalism, 29–30
  and history, 18, 19
Equality, and commercial republics, 28
Estates General, 121, 127, 130
Ethics, 133–134, 135. *See also* Morals
Europe
  and commerce, 92
  in feudalism, 90–91
  republics of, 100–102

Fact, idea of, 135–136
Federation, 93, 101, 105
Ferguson, Adam, 19, 20, 26, 29, 30, 48, 52
  on division of labor, 49
  on primitive life, 53
Fersen, 13n
Feudalism
  formation of, 90

INDEX

Feudalism (*Continued*)
  in Italy, 99
  and Marx, 32
  nature of, 21, 29–31, 85
  power under, 102
Feuillants Club, 10, 13, 14, 15, 40, 42, 61, 61n
Finances, French, 126–127
Flemish republics, 99–100
Florence, Republic of, 101
Foreign policy, of France, 6–9, 129
France
  commerce of, 141
  creditors of, 147–148
  government of, 120–121
  and hoarding, 149
  luxury in, 142–143
  in New World, 6–9
Freedom, sense of, 24, 25
French Revolution, 60–62
  causes of, 86, 122–128
  influences on, 128–131
  overview of, 75–76.
  See also Revolution
Friends of the Blacks (Amis des Noirs), 6, 7, 8
Frisch, M. H., 49n

Geneva, 100
Geography
  and commerce, 82
  and political systems, 85, 113, 122–123
Germany, monarchy of, 112–113
Girvonde Group, 39
Godechot, Jacques, 63n
Government
  in early society, 81
  finances, 148–150
  formation of, 76–77, 96
  French, 123–124, 128–131
Grégoire, Abbé, 6, 10, 39
Guizot, François, 64

Hanseatic towns, 100
Hébertistes, 58
Hegel, Georg, 68–69
Helvétius, Claude Adrien, 19, 40, 124, 133

Henry II, king of France, 120
Henry IV, king of France, 120, 149
Herder, Johan Gottfried von, 44, 48, 49n
Hindostan, empire of, 84
Hippocrates, 134
History, 17–22, 24, 27. *See also* Historiography
Historiography, 44–45
Hoarding, 148–150
Hobbes, Thomas, 47, 136
Hobsbawn, E. J., 32n
Holland, 103, 105, 129. *See also* United Provinces
House of Lords, 118–119
Hubert, René, 36n
Humanism, 41, 44
Hume, David, 18, 19, 25, 26, 40, 47, 48
Hungary, 112–114

Ideology, limitations of, 63–64
Industry, 68, 91, 98
Institutions, political, 77–78, 82. *See also* Government
Italy, Republic of, 98–99, 101

Jacobin Club, 6, 8, 61, 61n
Jaurès, Jean, 1–2, 4, 7n, 60, 64

Knowledge, aristocracy of, 78

Labor
  division of, 49, 58, 59, 67
  in early societies, 78–80
  property and wealth, 85, 92
Lacedemon, Republic of, 102
Lafayette, Marquis de, 40
Land
  and aristocracy, 85
  in society, 78–80, 92. *See also* Property
Laski, Harold, 2n
Laurent, E., 11n
Laws, 76–77 82, 83, 96
Lefebvre, Henri, 60
Legislator, role of, 68
Léon, Pierre, 2n

INDEX

Leopold II, emperor of Austria, 13
Liberty
    creation of, 93–94
    in Italy, 99
    and taxation, 145
Linguet, Nicholas, 59
Locke, John, 49
Logographe, 61
London, city of, 118
Lough, John, 2n
Louis XI, king of France, 120
Louis XIII, king of France, 120–121
Louis XIV, king of France, 120, 121, 123
Louis XV, king of France, 123, 125
Louis XVI, king of France, 123, 124, 126–127
Luther, Martin, 95, 97
Luxury, idea of, 25–26, 66, 68

Mably, 19, 40, 56
Mandeville, 25, 47, 52
Manufacturing, growth of, 81–82
Marat, Jean Paul, 58
Maritime Provinces, and democracy, 100, 115–118
Marx, Karl, 21n, 31–33, 58, 60, 65, 65n, 66, 67–68, 69. *See also* Marxism
Marxism, beginnings of, 64–65
Materialism, 21, 31–32, 70
Matheiz, 60
Mavidal, J., 11n
Mechanical arts, 35–36
    in development of society, 95, 98
    in Europe, 89, 91, 92
    means of wealth and power, 80, 82, 84, 85
Medici, family of, 101
Meinecke, Friedrich, 44
Merchant, as prototype of bourgeoisie, 143, 144
Michon, George, 1n, 4n
Militia, nature of, 107–108. *See also* Armed Forces
Millar, John, 19, 29
Mirabeau, Comte de, 6, 9–10
Modernity, sense of, 46–49
Monarchy
    in Asia, 84

    constitutional, 57, 68, 71
    culture of, 50–51
    in early societies, 78–79, 81
    in Europe, 85, 86, 89
    formation of, 94
    in France, 124–125, 128–129
    in inland states, 112–115
    in maritime states, 115–121
    nature of, 23–24, 25, 27–28, 43, 106–111
    power of, 90, 102
Montagnards, 72
Montaigne, Michel Eyquem de, 136
Montesquieu, 19, 20, 25, 39, 44, 46, 49, 52–53, 66, 69
    on aristocracy, 23–24, 26–27
    on feudalism, 29–30
    on modernity, 48
    on monarchy, 111–112
Morals
    in commercial states, 142–143
    in civil society, 96
    in democracy, 67
    and revolution, 141
    in science, 133–136
Morrow, G. R., 48n
Mounier, J. J., 38, 42

Naples, 115
Nature, 90, 91, 136
Navy, 104. *See also* Armed Forces
Necker, Jacques, 126n, 130n
New World, 6–9, 96, 116–117
Norway, 114

Optimism, eighteenth century, 38, 54

Palmer, R. R., 63n
Papacy, decline of, 85. *See also* Roman Catholic Church
Parlement of Paris, 121
Peter the Hermit, 95
Pétion, 10, 39
Philip II, king of Spain, 117
Philosophy
    in eighteenth century, 42–44, 45, 54, 137–138
    in France, 123
    and history, 17–22

INDEX

Physiocracy, 21, 36–37, 38. *See also* Physiocrats
Physiocrats, 40, 58. *See also* Physiocracy
Poland, monarchy of, 112–113, 115n
Popov-Lensky, I. L., 3n
Population, effects of, 78, 95, 96
Portugal, 116
Positivism, philosophy of, 44–46
Power
  in antiquity, 83, 84
  aristocratic and democratic, 23
  basis of, 76–77
  in commercial republics, 103
  in early societies, 78–83
  under feudalism, 77
  sources of, 101, 102
  and taxation, 145
Progress, the idea of, 28–35, 45, 47–50, 86–89
Property
  aristocratic, 22, 85
  and commerce, 20
  concept of, 38, 58, 70
  in early societies, 78–80
  under feudalism, 31, 90
  and industrial-commercial society, 92, 93
  and power, 77–78, 82
Prussia, monarchy of, 114
Public opinion, 28, 77, 95

Quinney, V. Y., 4n

Rationalism, Cartesian, 49. *See also* Reason
Raynal, 19, 40, 56
Reason, 36, 54–55, 91, 136–137. *See also* Causality
Reformation, 21
Religion, 41, 42, 95–96, 121
Renaissance, 53–54
Republics, formation of, 86, 103–105
Republicanism, 11, 27
Revolution
  causes of, 82, 86
  effects of, 85
  and history, 20
  and morals, 141. *See also* American Revolution; French Revolution
Revolutionary Tribunal, 13, 16, 72n
Richelieu, Cardinal, 120, 123
Right, idea of, 135. *See also* Ethics
Robertson, William, 19
Robespierre, Maximilien, 10, 39, 40, 58, 63–64, 72n
Roland, Madame, 39
Roman Catholic Church, 97–98. *See also* Clergy, Papacy
Roman Empire, 102, 130, 142–143
Rouché, Max, 49n
Rousseau, J.-J., 19, 21, 25, 38, 51, 59, 124
  personality description of, 138–140
Royer-Collard, 2n
Rude, Ferand, 1n, 75
Russia, state of, 114

Saint-Just, 58
Sans-culottes, 57, 58, 60
Santo Domingo, island of, 6, 7, 8
Schiller, Friedrich, 54–55
Science, 91, 133–136
Sentiment, and reason, 54–55
Sicily, kingdom of, 115
Sièye, 59
Slavery, 8, 20, 26
Smith, Adam, 19, 28, 37, 38, 40, 47–48, 49
Soboul, Albert, 60
Social class, concept of, 62
Society
  agricultural, 20–22, 33, 79–80, 89
  hunting, 20, 77
  industrial-commercial, 20, 23, 25–27
  pastoral, 20, 21, 26, 33, 79–80. *See also* Civil society
Söderhjelm, Alma, 4n
Spain, kingdom of, 116–117
Speculative mind, 135–136
Stendhal, 70
Steuart, James, 26
Strafford, Earl of, 42

Stuarts, of England, 120
Sweden, kingdom of, 114
Switzerland, republic of, 100, 102, 114

Tarquins, of Rome, 83
Taxation, 83, 144–146
Taylor, George V., 60n
Thierry, 64
Third Estate, 59, 124–125, 128–129
Tiberius, 124
Tocqueville, Alexis de, 30n
Towns, in history, 80, 99
"Triumvirs," of France, 9, 10, 13
Tudors, of England, 120
Tuileries, 16
Turgot, 20, 29, 34, 36–38, 44, 48, 57–58

United Provinces, 100. *See also* Holland

Venice, city of, 103–104
Vermale, F., 1n
Vico, Giambattista, 48, 49
Violence, historical, 29, 31, 32–33, 34–35
Voltaire, 18, 19, 25, 26, 42
Vyverberg, Henry, 47n

War, 34, 35, 109, 148–149
Warrior, as prototype of nobility, 143
Wealth
    in civil society, 85, 92, 95, 96
    in commercial republics, 98, 102, 103
    in early societies, 77–78, 81–83
Weulersse, George, 58n

Augsburg College
George Sverdrup Library
Minneapolis, Minnesota 55404